Sustaining G(

By Rodney Burton

Contributor: Rodney Burton
Editors & Previewers: Aaron Brockman, Gobel Brockman, Kim Burton, Rodney Burton, John Carnett, Gary J. Blanchard, Jacy Shelton
Cover design: Rodney Burton
Cover Artwork: Layout design courtesy of CreateSpace. Image courtesy of Public Domain.
Printed in the United States of America

ISBN-13: 978-149523535
ISBN-10: 149523553X

All Bible verses are the "New American Standard" version of the Bible unless otherwise noted.

I just finished reading Rodney's Burton's latest book, "Sustaining God's Presence" and I must say that I believe this should be considered a text book on how to keep the presence of God in one's life and Church. As a pastor, and revivalist, I am fully aware that it is much easier to "get" the presence of God to come, but much more difficult to keep or maintain it. A good comparison is, "it is easier to get married than it is to stay married." We can say we want Him in our lives, but then we balk at the price tag His presence carries. Salvation is free to all, but the depths of His presence and blessings in your life that it brings, is in relation to what you are willing to do to keep it. I will certainly recommend this book to others who are in pursuit of His presence.

Pastor Phillip Corbett
Author of "Running With Your Second Wind"

In "Sustaining God's Presence," Pastor Rodney Burton attempts to show how to keep close to God after the last mountaintop experience has worn off. Throughout the book, his pastor's heart for whoever is reading the book is clearly evident. He is obviously trying to reach and teach first and trying to write a book second. While no single element of his book bedazzles, I was impressed with how solid his writing is in every dimension. So, I'm giving him 5 stars on the all-around solidness of his work. His pastor's heart for readers is solid. His grasp of the breadth, depth, and humility of approach to the Scriptures is solid. His attention to the prose, font and legibility of the book is solid. The effectiveness of his book is solid. His use and timing of both Scriptural and personal stories is quite good (and solid). His theology is solid and flows from what he has learned and not what he thinks he knows.

Ron Leonard
Author of "Discerning Truth in a World Filled with Lies"

Dedication

To my wonderful Lord and Savior, Jesus Christ, not only the inspiration for this book, but the inspiration for my life.

To my wonderful and loving wife, Kim, who gives me the strength, courage, and encouragement to keep going, no matter how difficult things may seem or become.

To my wonderful son, Josiah, who inspires me daily. My prayer is that he would always know that all of his dreams can become a reality if he trusts God and applies what God has given to him.

To the congregations we have served in our ministry assignments in Indiana, Missouri, and Kentucky.

To the wonderful individuals and families of Calvary Church in Carthage, Illinois, where my family and I have the privilege of serving as pastors. As we continue to dig for and pursue God's best, I am reminded how blessed we are to have such a wonderful group on the journey with us.

This book is also dedicated to my mom and dad who continue to inspire me with the legacy they left behind for their family.

About the Author

Rodney Burton, along with his wife Kim, and son Josiah, currently serve as lead pastors of Calvary Church in Carthage, Illinois. Rodney and Kim are graduates of the Brownsville Revival School of Ministry in Pensacola, Florida. Rodney is ordained with the Assemblies of God. Their heart is to see the church come alive with the power, the presence, and the fullness of God. They feel the church has been living far below her potential and is in great need of a mighty move of God. Rodney's heart, his preaching, and his writing are driven by this passionate belief. You can learn more about the Burtons by visiting www.rodneyburton.net or their church website www.calvarychurchag.com.

Rodney's other published works:

"31 Keys to Possessing Your Promise"

"Carrying the Torch for Revival" (with Tom Stamman)

"Just Keep Digging"

Table of Contents

Dedication 3

About the Author...5

Foreword 7

Introduction 8

Chapter 1: Heart...11

Chapter 2: Hospitality 21

Chapter 3: Hunger...35

Chapter 4: Honor 47

Chapter 5: Humanity..57

Chapter 6: Humility 67

Chapter 7: Honesty 76

Chapter 8: Holiness 85

Chapter 9: Harmony...95

Chapter 10: Hope...105

Conclusion 115

Foreword

The Old Testament Prophet Jeremiah had a strong word from God for Israel.

My people have committed two sins: They have forsaken me, the spring of living water, and have dug their own cisterns, broken cisterns that cannot hold water. Jeremiah 2:13 (NIV)

In a day when many churches *dig their own cisterns* by trying to be trendy and relevant in order to satisfy the consumerism of church shoppers, Rodney Burton stands out as a prophetic voice reminding us of our need for God's presence.

Rodney is a product of the Brownsville Revival School of Ministry where he experienced the presence and power of God. Rodney was spoiled by those daily encounters and now lives with a passion to pursue more of God's daily presence.

The book you are reading is not formula driven. It is an invitation to live in God's daily presence. Rodney's engaging style and compelling illustrations bring clear exposition to walking and living with God. I invite you to not only read this book for enjoyment, but to read it devotionally and allow God to work in your life.

Gary Blanchard
Assistant Superintendent
Illinois District of the Assemblies of God

Introduction

My greatest desire is the presence of God. I am not interested in only an occasional visit by Him in some special moment or special service. I long for, desire, preach about, and pray for an abiding manifestation of His presence. In His presence is *fullness of joy.*[1] In the presence of the Lord is everything we could ever want or need. I have come to the place in my own life that I feel more comfortable in the presence of the Lord than I do out of His presence.

In December 1999, my wife and I graduated from the Brownsville Revival School of Ministry. We completed two years of associate's level study in the midst of the greatest revival of our generation. I am not going to declare that everything was perfect, as that is only possible in Heaven. Nonetheless, we were forever ruined by any level of life, church, or ministry void of God's presence and manifestation of power. That daily encounter with Him is what we consider to be completely normal Christianity. Since the time of our graduation we have experienced moments where we personally were back in that place of His abiding presence, but even that has not been enough for her or me. There is not one doubt in our minds that there is more, and we know that more is found nowhere else but in His presence.

My pursuit is not revival. My pursuit is not special meetings. My pursuit is not that which can be labeled, deciphered, or understood. My pursuit is Him and the place of His abiding presence. My pursuit is that which Obed Edom experienced when the Ark of the Covenant was left at his home when David first tried to move it back to Jerusalem. That

---

[1] Psalm 16:11

experience mightily impacted his life, he sold everything he owned, he went to Jerusalem to serve, and he was willing to do anything that would place him near the Ark. Yet it was not the Ark that drew him. It was the presence of God represented by and contained within the Ark. That is my pursuit. I want His presence. Nothing will bring about the lasting, eternal impact like His presence.

One moment in the presence of the Lord will do more than a lifetime of sermons or books written on the subject. One encounter with God will empower spirits, discomfort flesh, and destroy demons. Imagine with me, then, what His abiding presence will do. Dream with me. Choose to pursue a place of habitation with God, and not just a moment of visitation from Him. Can you dream for, plan for, and pursue that place?

If so this book is for you. The Lord has riveted me personally with this message time and again. This book contains what I am calling ten keys to sustaining God's presence. I do not pretend to believe this is an exhaustive list. There are many things that will sustain Him and many things that will push Him away. What this book is designed to explore are what I consider the foundational elements or characteristics that will both welcome and sustain God's presence in your life, your home, your family, your church, and everywhere you go.

I have tried to make this message simple by starting each key with the letter "H." The chapters or keys do not necessarily appear in any order of importance or preference, and they do not necessarily need to be read in any particular order. During the time of writing this book I have been challenged by different keys at different times. There were moments when the challenge for me was difficult, and I found myself wanting to remove that key altogether. Throughout the entire process, however, I have discovered the value of each of these things and have seen their impact in my own life. There are keys I will personally continue to work on at various times beyond this writing. I am nowhere near a master of any of these characteristics.

Something tells me this book will include future revisions and updates. I could even foresee additional keys being added. For now, however, you hold these ten for starters. My prayer is simple. May one, two, or all ten of these keys be used to unlock the sustaining power of God's presence in your own life as well as my own. I hope to hear your story soon about how God's presence impacts your life. From one pursuer of His presence to another, I hope we find Him together. If you are ready, let us make room for Him, open our hearts to Him, and hunger for Him. Let us pursue Him at all cost and be the spark through which His presence changes the world in which we live.

God bless,

Rodney

Chapter 1: Heart

Before we ever understand what it means to sustain God's presence, there must first be a desire in our hearts for His presence. We will never pursue or desire to sustain that for which we have no passion.

It does not take long to find out that for which we are passionate. A simple look at our schedule or checkbook will prove quite revealing. The Bible declares that *where your treasure is, there will your heart be also (Matthew 6:21).* This often quoted verse takes on a whole new meaning when considered within the context of what Jesus says in Matthew 6. Jesus tells us to not be caught up in other things and allow them to take priority over what is truly important – His Kingdom. Christ truly deserves the place of preeminence in our hearts. He belongs as the source and outlet of our love and worship. Is He our treasure? Consider these words from the Apostle Paul to the Corinthians:

*And even if our gospel is veiled, it is veiled to those who are perishing, in whose case the god of this world has blinded the minds of the unbelieving so that they might not see **the light of the gospel of the glory of Christ**, who is the image of God. For we do not preach ourselves but Christ Jesus as Lord, and ourselves as your bond-servants for Jesus' sake. For God, who said, "Light shall shine out of darkness," is the One who has shone in our hearts to give the Light of the knowledge of the glory of God in the face of Christ. But **we have this treasure in earthen vessels,** so that the surpassing greatness of the power will be of God and not from ourselves . . . 2 Corinthians 4:3-7*

Here we find real treasure – the person and glory of Jesus Christ. Many things in this life will try to distract us and keep us from seeing, realizing, or embracing this treasure. The god of this world will blind the eyes of the unbelieving so that their hearts will not come alive in Christ. A heart that is in the right place with Christ, however, is one that has realized the value of the treasure He truly is, and their words and actions serve as an expression of their heart. This is necessary for sustaining God's presence.

No matter what we do for or become in Christ, the fact still remains that we are simply a vessel that God has chosen to allow to hold the treasure of His presence. Consider the story of Jesus turning the water to wine in John 2. He found six water pots and commanded they be filled with water. These water pots had little value in their natural state. They were merely available for Jesus to use. Their value changed, however, when they were filled with water that became wine. Their value changed because of what Christ did inside of them. They were still the same ordinary water pots, but they were being used by Christ to minister to the guests. They held the treasure that Christ placed inside of them, and it was a blessing to everyone who was able to taste what had been given to them.

Christ desires and deserves to be the central focus of our hearts and lives. Far too many live half-heartedly toward Christ. He is our source of life, and not simply a by-product of religion. Everything we have in Him boils down to relationship with Him, and that relationship is a matter of our passion and heart. In his book of sermons from the Brownsville Revival, Evangelist Steve Hill shares this thought from a sermon entitled, *"The Fellowship of the Uncommitted."*[2]

_____

[2] *The God Mockers* by Stephen Hill, page 85.

If you are in the Armed Forces and you are uncommitted to the
service, you will be discharged. If you are a student and are
uncommitted to your studies, you will flunk out. Married person, if
you are uncommitted to your mate, you are headed for a divorce.
If you're a stockbroker who is uncommitted to your client, you will
go broke. If you are a doctor and are uncommitted to your
patients, they'll look for a physician who cares. If you are a lawyer
and are uncommitted to the law, you will be disbarred. If you are
a football player and are uncommitted to the team, you will be cut.
If you are a waiter and you're uncommitted to your table, you will
be tipless. If you are a Christian and you are uncommitted to
Christ, you are heading for serious judgment.

Our hearts must be committed to Him. We can quickly know and understand what is important in the life of an individual. That for which they are passionate will find expression. I have a five year old son who is quite passionate about Mario Brothers video games. Quite often I am asked to join him in an attempt to rescue Peach. If you were to watch him play I dare say you would be amazed at the intent and focus with which he approaches the game. He plays as though everything depends on the next move. He has a genuine passion for defeating Bowzer. In response to his passion, he puts his entire heart into the game. He is overjoyed when victorious. He is devesated when unsuccessful.

None of us is any different. We each can think of something for which we have a driving passion. The truth is that these passions, as long as they are not inherently sinful, are a normal part of life. It is healthy to be passionate. That is how our Father in Heaven has created us, for He is that passionate about all of His creation, especially you and me. When we are able to return to Him His level of passion for us, it is then when great fruit and life is produced in His presence.

One of the main problems I see within the Body of Christ, however, is misplaced or misguided passions. We spend far too much time in pursuit of things that have no genuine or eternal value. We stay busy chasing empty dreams, but missing out on the life-transforming power of God's presence. Even church itself can quickly become a combination of programs and ideas designed to arouse the senses of the congregation, while unable to penetrate their hearts. This leads to a continuous cycle of passionless believers. I pray God change that in all of our hearts.

Consider this cycle. Our passion and desire for God stirs the compassion in His heart that He has toward us. God's compassion always leads to God's passion and power. How many times in the Gospels do we read about Jesus being moved with compassion and healing someone? His compassion is strong and it is aimed at the needs in our lives. If we do not approach Him with a heart that desires His presence, however, He is often unable to release that compassion for us.

The compassion of Christ can be translated or understood as bowels of mercy. It may be said that He is full of compassion that is in need of release. That compassion is for you, but if you choose to go on in your own strength and never go to Him for or with your need, He will be unable to release that compassion on your behalf. If I may say it as bluntly as possible, our lack of heart and passion can render Christ constipated in His bowels of mercy. He has much for you and me, but unless we approach Him with a heart of passion and desire there is not much He can do to release all that He has available.

The real beauty, however, is to realize that the depths of compassion for us in the heart of Christ is just that – for us. His compassion and love is shown first to us and then to our needs. Far too often we assume if He cares enough about the need we

14

present He may do something on our behalf. He always cares deeply for us. When He walked the earth and stepped into the region known as Nain, He encountered a funeral procession. Everyone remembers the outcome of the story: Jesus raised the widow's son to life. Obviously that is the powerful climax of the story as recorded by Luke. We would be remiss, however, if we missed something just as powerful that happens even before He raises the young man from the dead. Consider these words carefully:

When the Lord saw her, He felt compassion for her, and said to her, "Do not weep." Luke 7:13

Jesus was moved with compassion for the woman herself even before He dealt with the need in her life. This woman was a widow who had just experienced the death of her only son. She was in a difficult social and economic position. There was a great sense of hopelessness and helplessness surrounding her, and Jesus recognized that and responded. This particular miracle is unique in that we do not find the woman seeking out or calling on Jesus with her need. What we do find is the level and depth of compassion Jesus feels toward humanity. He was drawn to this widow and before He raised her son, He touched her life. This pictures the heart that God has toward you and me. He is passionate about us. He is concerned for us and not just for our needs.

That heart sustained the power, presence, and authority of God's Kingdom throughout the ministry of Jesus Christ. He was able to speak with compassion and authority toward the widow when He told her to stop weeping. I hear Him declaring to her, *Daughter do not weep. Do not allow the circumstances of life to suck the life out of you, because Life itself is standing before you now!* The passion and compassion in His heart brought the manifestation of the presence of God in and through His life. When Jesus spoke life to the son in the casket there was no question what was going to transpire. Out of the abundance of His heart His mouth spoke. Life was contained in His heart and therefore life came forth from His mouth. Death had no choice but to leave.

Let God Search the Heart

Jeremiah declared that *the heart is more deceitful than all else and is desperately sick; who can understand it? I, the Lord, search the heart.*[3] When left unsearched or unchecked our hearts are deceitful and sick. But the Lord searches the heart. When He does so, He brings healing and life. Out of that new heart, what Ezekiel refers to as a heart of flesh[4], comes life, passion, and that which can sustain the abiding presence of God.

Our natural tendency is to gravitate toward that which is appealing or pleasing to our own self. Our heart is considered *deceitful* because it is often connected to and directed by our fleshly nature. In terms of temptation and sin we often imply that the devil made us do it; truthfully it is of our own choosing. James declares that *each one is tempted when he is carried away and enticed by his own lust.*[5] It emanates from our own desires, from our own hearts. We are naturally bent that direction. As James continues, the end result of that temptation and lust is death. If our hearts are not made alive in Christ they are destined for death. I love these words written by David.

---

[3] Jeremiah 17:9-10

[4] Ezekiel 36:26

[5] James 1:14

Search me, O God, and know my heart; try me and know my anxious thoughts; and see if there be any hurtful way in me, and lead me in the everlasting way. Psalm 139:23-24

The Psalmist entreats God to search his heart and to make his sinful ways known to him. He knows that if left to itself his heart's tendency is toward that which is evil. Do not mistake the wording here. On their own, our thoughts are anxious. How often do we think and act based on anxiety, stress, or emotion? How many times do we find ourselves being tossed about and driven by what we feel or perceive? In that place it is extremely difficult to recognize or sustain the presence of God. In Mark 4, the disciples were in the boat with Jesus when the storm arose. They were anxious in their thoughts as the storm began to rage. They became fearful, not because of the storm, but because in that moment they lost sight of Who was in the boat with them. The anxiety and emotion brought on by circumstances of life should never be seen as bigger than Jesus. Outward pressures cannot defeat the inward peace found in His presence. When our hearts and minds are stayed upon Him, He promises to keep us in perfect peace.[6]

The Psalmist also declares that his ways are hurtful. Our ways are naturally hurtful. Our ways hurt God. It was our ways that caused the need for a perfect sacrifice, found only in the death of Jesus Christ. Our ways hurt people. All of the things in my life that I would like to take back involve hurt I have caused someone else. Our ways hurt ourselves. A person's character can take a lifetime to build, a moment to destroy.

The point is that we all need to allow God to search and keep our hearts in check, and we need it done daily. My heart may be good today, but it may easily be deceitful tomorrow. I

[6] Isaiah 26:3

cannot rely on the heart of God that I possessed and displayed yesterday. Today is a new day. His mercy is new every morning, and I stand as one in need of a heart check on a daily basis. Otherwise, I may quickly find myself slipping away from and distancing myself from His presence.

Our Passion is for Him

To others your passion for God is either appealing or it is appalling. To God it is always a delight. When David brought the Ark back to Jerusalem, he was dancing and celebrating before the Lord, and it was appalling to Michal, his wife. The Bible declares that *she despised him in her heart.*[7] Her feelings were deep enough that she confronted David about his display of passion when he returned home that evening. His response to her gives clear insight regarding the purpose of passion for God.

So David said to Michal, "It was before the Lord, who chose me above your father and above all his house, to appoint me ruler over the people of the Lord, over Israel; therefore I will celebrate before the Lord. 2 Samuel 6:21

David did not dance with passion before the public so that they would hold him in higher esteem. He was already the king. Michal argued that his actions could prove detremintal. Yet David declared, *It was before the Lord.* This should be the motivation for our actions. I do not display my own passion in my worship, in my preaching, or in my writing for the sake of man or his approval. Yes, many of the things I do are *before* man but they are not *for* man. The greatest display of passion that I show toward God is done in private. If I make my passion for Christ a public spectacle then I have determined to make it more about me than about Him. The plan of God will begin to unfold

---

[7] 2 Samuel 6:16

when we realize it is bigger than us. When centered on us, we miss God's purpose and plan.

I have seen my share of individuals who long to be recognized and heralded for their displays of spirituality. They dance or react in hopes that everyone is watching. I have watched it time and again and it always saddens me. We have this saying at our church: If someone has a deep desire for the praise and recognition of man they need only ask me. I will help them fulfill that need. We will take a moment and parade them in front of everyone. If desired, we will prepare four strong men to carry them on an elevated chair. We might even be able to convince the worship team to deliver a powerful rendition of "How Great Thou Art." If that is the sincere motivation then we can play to that soulish and selfish desire. Obviously I say this tongue in cheek, as I should never genuinely do these things.

On the flip side is the beautiful picture of one lost in the presence of the Lord, with intent to worship Him. I have a friend named Josh with whom I went to Bible school at Brownsville. Today Josh pastors a church in Ohio. One of my favorite things to do during worship time at Brownsville was to locate Josh and see his genuine passion for Jesus. He might strangle me for writing this about him, but we are far enough away geographically that I feel safe. One night that truly stands out in my mind is when Josh was hiding in the balcony of the church. He was up there with his handkerchief, dancing and worshiping God with all his might. He was neither putting on a show nor seeking the approval of man. His worship was unto and before the Lord. I doubt he knows I saw him. I doubt he knows I remember, yet it made an impression on me.

When that which we offer to the Lord comes from a pure heart, God will inhabit that offering of praise with His abiding presence. What more could we possibly want? Man's opinion and approval may bring temporary excitement, but God's presence brings eternal value. And the beauty is that it is never about the size of that which we offer to Him. Jesus commended the woman who offered the two small coins, for she had given of all she had.[8] Often we feel what we have to offer is insignificant, but God loves to receive from a heart that is purely devoted to Him.

When asked what was the greatest commandment, the answer of Jesus was both simple and profound.

And He said to him, "You shall love the Lord your God with all your heart, and with all your soul, and with all your mind. This is the great and foremost commandment."
Matthew 22:37-38

Before we do anything else, we are to love the Lord with all of our heart. Out of that everything else related to the Kingdom flows. Access to the Kingdom and the presence of God comes through giving your heart to Jesus. Sustaining the presence of God happens by keeping your heart devoted to Him. He does not just want a one time or an occasional gift of your heart. We must not approach Him as an annual Valentine. He desires the full commitment of our hearts at all times, and His presence is worth that ongoing investment.

---

[8] Mark 12:41-44

Chapter 2: Hospitality

Have you ever walked into a place and immediately felt that you were not welcome? It is definitely an uncomfortable feeling. One night, following a late service at our church with a guest evangelist, we were going out to eat. There were going to be ten or twelve of us together for the meal, therefore we chose a nearby place that was open twenty-four hours and could easily accommodate our group. My wife (fiancée at the time) and I were the first to arrive. When the hostess asked how many in our party she was clearly appalled by our answer. I can still hear her relaying the information to the kitchen, and then hearing the reply from the kitchen. Due to crude and harsh language alone I will not quote the response from the kitchen. We were clearly not welcome.

I was tired and chose to go home. The rest of the group found another place that was more than happy to serve them and earn their business. The next day my father-in-law visited the manager of the unwelcoming restaurant to make him aware of the lack of hospitality we had received. He took along the receipt from the restaurant that did accommodate the group. The restaurant manager was given a clear picture of the value of hospitality.

The same rings true in terms of our being hospitable toward God. We stand to lose many benefits of His presence if we choose to not welcome Him in His fullness.

Welcome to Dwell

Elisha was God's chosen prophet in his day. A read-through his life as recorded in 2 Kings reveals many great things accomplished through his life and ministry. He was well known, highly respected, and greatly feared as a man who represented God powerfully. In the fourth chapter of 2 Kings we read the story of Elisha and the Shunammite woman. The first time Elisha passed through Shunem, a *prominent woman* met him and provided him something to eat. It became customary that any time Elisha would pass through the area; he would eat food at the home of this woman and her husband. He became a frequent visitor at their place.

Elisha was more than a visitor to this family. After one of Elisa's visits we find the woman sharing her feelings with her husband in the following manner:

"Behold now, I perceive that this is a holy man of God passing by us continually. Please, let us make a little walled upper chamber and let us set a bed for him there, and a table and a chair and a lampstand; and it shall be, when he comes to us, that he can turn in there." 2 Kings 4:10-12

The Shunammite woman determined that she was going to be hospitable toward the man of God. Throughout this chapter Elisha will serve as a type of God Himself. I want us to see that the Shunammite woman was ultimately making room for God. Her approach and plan was specific. When we determine that God's presence is worth being sustained and not just entertained, we will find ourselves making plans to accommodate Him in an ongoing manner.

When you realize that they made a special room for Elisha, you begin to understand the significance of hospitality. The room was not designed haphazardly. The Shunammite woman and her husband had learned some things about Elisha, and that knowledge led to specific items being placed in his special room. It seems quite apparent that during his times of visitation, the couple had spent time with Elisha and therefore understood what needed to be done to accommodate him for a longer period of time. The desire behind the room was *when he comes to us that he may turn in there.* The room was therefore designed in a way that would make that desire a reality. They did not place him outside of their home, they added room in their home to accommodate the abiding presence of the man of God.

The motives of the Shunammite woman were pure. She was looking to be a blessing to God and not to be blessed by God. Regardless of anything else we do, if our motives are wrong our actions will lose their meaning. Never once do we read of Elisha asking for a meal or for a special room. This woman simply saw a need and an opportunity to be hospitable toward the man of God. When it came time to design the room she wanted to be sure that it created an atmosphere that was welcoming.

A Bed

The first thing we find placed inside the room was a bed. The bed represents a place where the presence of God (as represented by Elisha) may rest. A bed is not something you make available to dinner guests; a bed is something you make available to those you desire to stay for an extended period of time. Without the bed in the room, it would have not truly given the message of welcome. No bed in the room would have indicated Elisha was welcome to check out the room but not to check in to the room.

Before anything else went into the room there was a bed. The first thing that must happen in our desire to be hospitable toward the presence of the Lord is that we must ensure we make room for His presence to rest. In Genesis 8, Noah employed a dove to help determine the end of the flood. He let the dove fly from the ark to see if the land was dry. When the dove returned back to him it was obvious that the bird had found no place to rest as a result of the floodwaters. On the third trip the dove never returned. The floodwaters had receded and the dove found a place to rest.

Noah understood that a dove would look to find a place that was inhabitable. The dove would fly in search of more than just a spot to land. The dove would be in search of a place to dwell. Is that not a perfect picture of the Holy Spirit? He is not simply looking for a place to land or visit. He is looking for a place that is inhabitable. When Jesus was baptized in water we are told the Holy Spirit descended on Him in the form of a dove.[9] In Christ, the Holy Spirit found a place to dwell.

By placing a bed in the room first the Shunammite woman was declaring that this room was a place Elisha was welcome to come and stay for as long as he desired. From her standpoint the longer he stayed the better it would be. There must have been something that had taken place during the times Elisha had visited and had eaten with them. There was a reason this woman desired to make room for Elisha to stay longer. My guess is that she enjoyed the blessing of hosting the presence that Elisha carried. I believe this woman and her husband had come to realize that their home was more peaceful, their crops were more fruitful, and whenever Elisha was around everything was generally better. If there was blessing in the visitation, imagine the possibilities if he became a dweller. What could happen if the presence of God lived in their home? What if they could sustain what they briefly experienced during the times Elisha would visit? They were making a decision to be hospitable and welcoming toward God's presence. It was a small step to sustaining all that came with God's presence.

---

[9] Matthew 3:16

A Table

Next we find that a table was placed in the room. First, the table represents a place where God may fellowship and spend family time with people. Secondly, the table represents a place where God may work. To sustain God's presence there needs to be both an atmosphere where God is able to genuinely spend time with us and an atmosphere where God is able to work with, on, and among us. The table fully embodies Lazarus' two sisters, Mary and Martha.

Now as they were traveling along, He entered a village; and a woman named Martha welcomed Him into her home. She had a sister called Mary, who was seated at the Lord's feet, listening to His word. But Martha was distracted with all her preparations; and she came up to Him and said, "Lord, do You not care that my sister has left me to do all the serving alone? Then tell her to help me." But the Lord answered and said to her, "Martha, Martha, you are worried and bothered about so many things; but only one thing is necessary, for Mary has chosen the good part, which shall not be taken away from her." Luke 10:38-42

Mary was honored by Jesus because she was spending her time sitting at His feet, spending time with Him in His presence. For her the table would have been all about communion with Jesus. Many times in Scripture we find Mary in the same place – at the feet of Jesus. Martha, on the other hand, was busy working to host Jesus and all those who were with Him. For her the table represented a place of work. When we seek to be hospitable toward God's presence we must realize that He fully embodies both Mary and Martha. He is a God who delights in communion with His people, and He is a God who is a diligent worker both with and in His people.

By placing a table in the room, the Shunammite woman was at once providing the possibility of relationship and communion. She was also making it possible for Elisha to work. Proper balance here can keep us from the dangerous place of becoming too familiar with God's presence, causing us to lose our awe of His presence, and losing sight of the work that is done by His presence. It may be easy to become enamored with either God's presence or the way God works; we need both. I do not want Him to just work in my life or in our church. I want His presence to abide and to be manifest at all times. At the same time, however, I do not just want to know that He is present; I want to allow Him to work and to do what only He can do. The table allows for both.

A Chair

After the bed and the table we find that a chair was placed in the room prepared for Elisha. The chair represents a place where someone can feel at home. It spoke of a welcoming environment where one felt he could stay. I firmly believe the chair in place would have been quite comfortable and inviting. I can think of few things that make me want to leave a place more than a chair that is not comfortable. If the seat makes you fidgety or uncomfortable it will keep you from being at your best.

It is important that when we make room for God we ensure that He is comfortable. The message given must be that we want Him to feel at home, and therefore see no reason to look for somewhere else to go. I have an oversized rocker recliner in my living room that always welcomes me. When we first bought the new furniture I found myself falling asleep in that chair many nights. It made my wife wonder if it was too comfortable. Each time I sit in it I find myself being thankful for the decision to purchase the chair. I am confident that is what the Shunammite woman was going for with the chair for Elisha. Her desire was that Elisha would feel at home in the chair, and that it would draw him to the room. More than anything else in my life, and in our church, I want the atmosphere to be inviting to God. I want Him to feel drawn to come and to be with us.

I also believe the chair placed in the room would have been appropriate to Elisha's position and prestige. It would not have been a small, child-sized chair. It would have been a chair fitting for royalty, as in the days of Elisha a prophet was held in the highest regard. Ultimately we are talking about being hospitable to the King of the entire universe. We must, therefore, ensure that the chair is fitting for a king. The atmosphere must not only be inviting and welcoming, but it must also be honoring to God. If a person of natural royalty and prestige were to come into your home you would be sure to offer him or her the absolute best seat in the house. We should do no less with the King of kings.

By placing a chair in the room, the Shunammite woman was extending a comfortable and inviting place for Elisha to come and stay. It was her way of honoring his efforts, recognizing his authority, and allowing him to be at home. I understand that Heaven is God's natural home, and I believe we can do our part to make room for God that is as much of Heaven on Earth as possible.

A Lampstand

The final thing we find placed in the room was a lampstand. The lampstand represents having the light on and thus having the darkness dispelled. God is light and in Him there is no darkness. The lamp serves as a reminder of the importance of not allowing our light to become extinguished. This is all about recognizing and understanding who you are hosting. Plus, the light represents that which in inviting. Even a known motel chain offers to leave the light on to welcome you.

One thing that comes to mind from my childhood home is the front porch light. No matter how old I or any of my siblings became, if mom or dad knew we were going to be arriving after dark, the porch light would be on when we arrived. I can still hear my dad saying, "We'll leave the porch light on for you." It was a way of making sure we knew we were welcome. It was a way of making sure we could see clearly to find our way. Even though I could walk the sidewalk and porch in my sleep, having the light on meant there was someone on the inside who wanted to make sure I got inside safely. The front porch light meant that I was wanted and welcome.

Do we leave the light on for God? Do we keep the light of His gospel alive in our hearts in such a way that He can clearly see His way into the place in which we invite Him? There is absolutely nothing about God that would ever make Him unapproachable to us. We need to avoid the darkness and anything in our own lives that would make us unapproachable to Him.

By placing the lampstand inside of the room, the Shunammite woman was declaring her desire for the light to be greater than the darkness. The unwritten sign above the door of this room was *please stay here!* She and her husband were doing all that they could to make Elisha – the representation of God – feel welcome and desire to dwell. The more you and I desire for God to not just visit but to dwell, the more we will do to make the atmosphere welcoming to Him.

What Happens When We Welcome God's Presence?

The results and benefits of welcoming God's presence are immeasurable. I stated in *Just Keep Digging* that the destination pays the price of the journey.[10] It is important that we keep that same principle in mind as we choose to be hospitable toward God. The full extent of what transpires in God's presence is not always going to be easy, but the overwhelming benefit and value of God's presence covers all costs.

The room was designed for Elisha without an agenda or personal motive. The Shunammite did so out of a genuine heart that valued the presence of God. Even if we put all of the right things in place to prepare a room for God, our motive will trump our actions. If our hearts are not pure our actions become meaningless. Often we fail to receive from God because we approach Him with a hand of request rather than a hand of offering. Yet when our motives are pure, we experience God's blessing and favor in ways we could never expect.

The beautiful part of this story is that when Elisha asked this woman what he could do for her, she asked for absolutely nothing. She was extended an offer to ask for essentially anything she wanted. What she wanted was what she already had – God's presence dwelling in her home. When we make room for God, He extends all that is in Him – His mercy, grace, peace, joy, presence, Holy Spirit – toward us to enable us to live the abundant life He has made available. God, however, is gracious and merciful toward us, and He will not be denied His own desire to bless us. The woman's heart was in the right place, and she received a blessing that was above that which she could even think to ask.

---

[10] *Just Keep Digging* by Rodney Burton

So he said, "What then is to be done for her?" And Gehazi answered, "Truly she has no son and her husband is old." He said, "Call her." When he had called her, she stood in the doorway. Then he said, "At this season next year you will embrace a son." And she said, "No, my lord, O man of God, do not lie to your maidservant." The woman conceived and bore a son at that season the next year, as Elisha had said to her. 2 Kings 4:14-17

When our heart is into blessing and not being blessed, God will bestow a blessing upon us beyond our comprehension. What He gives to us is often even bigger than that for which we are even able to ask. He knows the deep desires of our heart, and when we make it a priority to make room for Him, He is able to bring even those things to life! Within a year this woman held in her arms the fruit of her own labor. When she chose to approach God as though she lacked nothing, He satisfied even that which was lacking in her life.

It is vitally important that after you make room for God, you do everything you can to continue to maintain that room for God, and protect His presence. As this story continues, and the Shunammite's son dies, she took her dead son into the room that had been prepared for God's presence. Often after God has blessed someone they go on their merry way, forgetting Him: then when crisis hits, they have nowhere to turn because they have not maintained the place for God's presence. The bottom line is that we do not create room for God so that He may bless us. We create room for God because nothing compares to His presence.

One day as he was out working with his father the young boy become sick and his sickness led to his death. The response of his mother tells us much about her character and her understanding of God's presence. The boy took his last breath in her arms, yet her reaction was unconventional. She took the boy and laid him on Elisha's bed. She was laying her need at the place where God rested.

She was able to lay the boy on the bed, because the room had not changed. How easy would it have been for this couple to turn Elisha's room into a nursery or bedroom for their son? Many times after we receive what we want or need from God we turn His room into something else. Then a need arises and we are not sure where to go or what to do.

When you are confident that you have made room for God's presence to rest then you will be able to leave your need at that place. After taking the boy and placing him on the bed, the Shunammite woman left to go to Elisha. She left her need where she laid her need. Also, when others inquired of her whether things were all right, she kept the information to herself until she got to where Elisha was and spoke to him. She had made room for Elisha, she had developed a relationship with him, and she understood that what he could do for her need was greater than what anyone else could do for the same need. Therefore, he was going to be the first one to whom she would speak.

From Elisha's response we see a picture of how God will respond to us as well. He gave his full attention to the woman, because he could recognize her desperation. The desperate cry of one in need will always capture the attention of God. When he arrived at the room, Elisha laid himself upon the dead body of the child. Because she had made room for him, because she had gone to him in her time of need, she got the fullness of Elisha in response to her need. This woman never wavered in her devotion toward God. She never wavered in giving her fullness to Him. As a result, she was blessed by having God's fullness applied to her need. When the fullness of life is applied to death there is only one possible outcome. The woman got her son back.

This is not the end of the story. When a person makes room for God and welcomes Him, He in turn makes room for them and provides blessing and protection. In the eighth chapter of 2 Kings, we find Elisha speaking to the Shunammite a word of caution about a coming time of famine. He told her to depart from her home, and dwell in another land in order to be protected from the famine. She was being prepared, protected, and provided for as a result of her hospitality toward God. We find that she spent seven years in the land of the Philistines, the nation often recognized as the enemy of Israel. In essence, she was provided for and protected in the land of the enemy. She and her household were blessed and honored by God.

At the end of the seven years of famine, the Shunammite returned to appeal to the king for her house and her land, hoping to have it restored. We see how God responds to those who are hospitable toward Him. God knows how to take care of His people. Listen to what the Word says next:

Now the king was talking with Gehazi, the servant of the man of God, saying, "Please relate to me all the great things that Elisha has done." As he was relating to the king how he had restored to life the one who was dead, behold, the woman whose son he had restored to life appealed to the king for her house and for her field. And Gehazi said, "My lord, O king, this is the woman and this is her son, whom Elisha restored to life." When the king asked the woman, she related it to him. So the king appointed for her a certain officer, saying, "Restore all that was hers and all the produce of the field from the day that she left the land even until now." 2 Kings 8:4-6

At the exact time this woman was going in to appeal to the king, the king was talking to Gehazi about all the things Elisha had done.   In the midst of sharing the story of the Shunammite woman, she and her son appear before the king to appeal for her land.   Not even Hollywood could write this script. Not only did she and her family receive their land back, but they were also given *all the produce of the field from the day that she left the land even until now.*   She was warned of the coming famine.   She was safe in the land of the Philistines.   She successfully appeared before the king at just the right time.   Her land was restored to her.   And she was given produce for which she had not labored during the seven years of famine.   God loves relationship, and the person who makes room for Him will enjoy great benefits of relationship with God.

From the beginning it has been the intention of God to spend time in relationship with His people.   The most devastating thing that happened in the Garden of Eden was the severing of that relationship.   When God came to walk with and spend time with them in the cool of the day, He found they were hidden because they had sinned.   From that time there have been steps taken to restore that opportunity for fellowship.   God is relational, and He desires to spend time with you and me.   He is looking for those who will make room for Him.   He will respond to our hospitality.   He desires to *dwell in them and walk among them;* with a desire to be *their God, and they shall be My people.*[11]

Through the work of Jesus Christ on the cross we have been granted blessed access to an intimate relationship with Him.   Are we willing to be as the Shunammite woman and make room for Him?   Are we willing to do so with a pure heart that is

---

[11] 2 Corinthians 6:16

motivated solely by a desire to be in His presence? Oh that we would all gain an unwavering understanding of the beauty and value of His presence in such a way that nothing else would compare. May we with the fervor of Isaiah cry for God to rend the Heavens and come down![12]

---

[12] Isaiah 64:1

Chapter 3: Hunger

Have you ever experienced a time in your life when you were deeply hungry for something? I will never forget a time when at the age of ten I thought I understood hunger. My nephew and I were seeing how long we could survive without eating, and we were starting to grow concerned when we had made it four hours. I recall the television being on and it seemed every commercial was about food. We were famished. Our lives were spared, however, when his mom returned from the grocery store. We quickly did major damage to a bag of potato chips. At last our deep hunger was satisfied.

Obviously going four hours without eating is nothing special. Yet there is something that takes place when you begin to take notice of hunger. There were other times when my nephew and I would have gone much longer without eating, but we had no reason to notice our hunger, because we were too busy focusing on other things.

When we do not allow other things to steal our focus, our hunger for God is able to maintain a place of priority in our lives. Jesus said it in this manner:

Blessed are those who hunger and thirst for righteousness, for they shall be filled. Matthew 5:6 (New King James)

This verse nestled in the heart of what we know to be the Beatitudes says a mouthful (pun intended). The word hunger in this context is used metaphorically, meaning to crave ardently or to seek with eager desire. The image painted by Christ is that you are desperately hungry for His righteousness, and you have determined nothing else will suffice. It is a specific and picky hunger.

Have you ever been hungry for a specific thing? Often when my wife asks me what I would like to have for lunch or dinner, my typical answer is that anything is fine. She does not particularly enjoy that answer, but I am being completely honest. In that moment there is not any one thing that stands out as the food object of my desire. There are occasions, however, when there is one thing that I have my mind, heart, and mouth set on to eat. Usually for me that one thing is steak. When that specific hunger happens, and conversely when that hunger is satisfied, I am a happy camper. There is something wonderful about consuming that for which you have a genuine hunger. In those times when nothing in particular sounds good, I still eat, and I still reach the point of being full; it just is not the same.

Jesus is calling us to the same thing in this statement. He wants us to have a specific and driving hunger for His righteousness. Far too often we have an appetite and attitude that anything will work for our spiritual nourishment. Those times of consuming other things may leave us feeling full, but they will keep us truly lacking. The begging question then is what is this righteousness for which Christ calls us to hunger?

As said in Matthew by Jesus, this righteousness speaks of *integrity, virtue, purity of life, uprightness, correctness in thinking, feeling, and acting.*[13] Jesus is calling for us to have a craving for these characteristics in our lives. We do not have the capacity within ourselves to produce these characteristics. These are the attributes of God for as Isaiah says, *our righteousnesses are like filthy rags.*[14] Jesus is calling us to hunger for the righteousness of God, and the way to find and sustain His righteousness is by

---

[13] www.interlinearbible.org

[14] Isaiah 64:6

being in His presence. Jesus therefore is calling us to hunger to be in God's presence.

I am intrigued by the following information regarding the foraging or eating behavior of sheep and goats.

A big difference between sheep and goats is their foraging behavior and diet selection. Goats are natural browsers, preferring to eat leaves, twigs, vines, and shrubs. They are very agile and will stand on their hind legs to reach vegetation. Goats like to eat the tops of plants. Sheep are grazers, preferring to eat short, tender grasses and clover. Their dietary preference is forbs (broadleaf weeds) and they like to graze close to the soil surface. Goats require a more nutritious diet.[15]

What I gather from this is that for sheep and goats their hunger seems specific to their needs or pursuits. Based on the simplicity of their diet, sheep seem content with what they have, they have found what works for them, and they are fine to continue to consume the same thing. Perhaps a primary reason many have a greater hunger for natural things than they do for God is because they have yet to discover the dietary benefit of consuming the things of God. Many goats are still searching for what works for them. It may be called "a more nutritious diet," but it is a broader yet less satisfying diet.

When Daddy Understands

I will never forget when the concept of hunger truly sunk in for me personally. Our son, Josiah, was born on September 16, 2008. We brought him home from the hospital on Thursday evening, September the 18th (my birthday☺). As you might guess, the first night home was a bit tough for him. The hardest

---

[15] www.sheep101.info

thing for me as his dad, however, was that there was a twelve to thirteen hour stretch on Friday that he did not eat. Kim would attempt to feed him and he had no interest. The pediatrician assured me that if Josiah seemed content, I should not become too concerned. I trusted our pediatrician 100%, but he still could not convince me to not be concerned.

I had to run a couple of errands that afternoon during the non-eating stretch. As I was going through town, I was praying about my son not eating, reminding God that it was vital. There have been times in my life where I have heard the Lord clearly speak to my heart. This was one of those times. He simply said to me,

I needed you to understand how a father feels when his child isn't eating.

I was completely captivated and taken aback at this point, because I expected something comforting from Him. In response, I began to repent of the times in my own life which I had not been eating spiritually. God had captured my attention in that moment and helped me to see the value of hunger. It bothers the heart of our Father in Heaven when we choose to not have spiritual appetite. Many in the church believe that we are fine as long as we are content, but contentment can quickly turn to complacency and spiritual starvation.

Josiah did begin eating that day, and he has eaten every day since then. In fact, as you may have guessed, he eats more as he grows. The spiritual application is the same. We cannot afford to see our hunger wane as we grow in our relationship with the Lord. Quite the opposite is true. As we grow in him, the growth is driven by our appetite for Him and our response to the hunger in our hearts. There are too many within the church that have tasted and seen that the Lord is good only to put down their utensil and quit eating. Let us never become content or satisfied to the point that we lose our hunger and desire for the Lord.

Consider Ephesus

In the Lord's address to the Seven Churches of Asia in Revelation chapters 2 and 3, He warns the Church of Ephesus that they had left their first love.[16] Their initial hunger for God had begun to wane. When Paul had first arrived in Ephesus he encountered twelve men who were praying.   During their discourse, these men became hungry for the things of God's Spirit and they were baptized in the Holy Spirit.[17] From there we read that Paul was in Ephesus preaching the Gospel in what many would consider a great revival. My favorite verse from this particular chapter of Acts is this:

This took place for two years, so that all who lived in Asia heard the word of the Lord, both Jews and Greeks. Acts 19:10

What a powerful statement to be made about an entire region hearing the Gospel. For the ministers who are reading this book, who among us would not want that to be said about the region in which we minister? It is also in Acts 19 where we read about the seven sons of Sceva and their attempt to cast the spirit out of the demoniac man. On the heels of that incident the public brought their magic art books and began to burn them. The Word of God was having great impact in the area, and God's Kingdom was growing in influence.

Nonetheless, in Revelation Jesus declared that the Church of Ephesus had forsaken their first love. Perhaps they had become too caught up in the cares of this world or religious

---

[16] Revelation 2:4

[17] Acts 19

duties which caused their hunger and passion to wane. A study of Ephesians, the letter to this church; as well as a study of First and Second Timothy, who served as the pastor of this church; may give some insight into the issues and challenges faced by these believers. The warning I hear loudly is that we must be careful that we do not allow anything in life to stand in the way of our hunger for God.

At the end of each of the seven letters in Revelation 2 and 3, Jesus gives a promise to those who overcome. In the conclusion of His letter to the Church of Ephesus, Jesus declares that the one who overcomes will be given the right *to eat of the tree of life which is in the Paradise of God*.[18] The symbolism to me is clear. If we do not allow ourselves to be drawn away and enticed by that which does not satisfy, we will be given the ultimate opportunity to consume from the Tree of Life. The prophet Isaiah says it in this manner:

"Ho! Every one who thirsts, come to the waters; and you who have no money come, buy and eat. Come, buy wine and milk without money and without cost. Why do you spend money for that which is not bread, and your wages for what does not satisfy? Listen carefully to Me, and eat what is good, and delight yourself in abundance." Isaiah 55:1-2

Hunger Placement

So often we find ourselves going after things that appeal to our flesh and feed an appetite that is going to profit us little. There is an old Native American Cherokee story that illustrates this:[19]

---

[18] Revelation 2:7

[19] www.firstpeople.us

One evening an old Cherokee told his grandson about a battle that goes on inside people. He said, "My son, the battle is between two wolves inside us all. One is Evil – It is anger, envy, jealousy, sorrow, regret, greed, arrogance, self-pity, guilt, resentment, inferiority, lies, false pride, superiority, and ego. The other is Good – It is joy, peace, love, hope, serenity, humility, kindness, benevolence, empathy, generosity, truth, compassion and faith." The grandson thought about it for a minute and then asked his grandfather: "Which wolf wins?" The old Cherokee simply replied, "The one you feed."

We do find our lives controlled by the side of us we nourish the most. In his letter to the Galatians, Paul says that the one who sows to the flesh will reap corruption, but the one who sows to the spirit will reap eternal life.[20] There really is an internal battle which forces us to decide how we will feed ourselves. This battle is not a one-time event either. We live with an ongoing struggle to feed either our flesh or our spirit. Smith Wigglesworth is quoted as saying, *"I find nothing in the Bible but holiness. I find nothing in the world but worldliness; therefore, if I live in the world I will become worldly. On the other hand, if I live in the Bible I will become holy."*

We have a mandate from Christ to *hunger and thirst after righteousness.*[21] It is easy, however, to find ourselves hungry and thirsty for many other things. I want to conclude this chapter with wise counsel from the book of Proverbs.

When you sit down to dine with a ruler, consider carefully what is before you, and put a knife to your throat if you are a man of great appetite. Do not desire his delicacies, for it is deceptive food. Do not weary yourself to gain wealth, cease from your consideration

---

[20] Galatians 6:8

[21] Matthew 5:6

of it. When you set your eyes on it, it is gone. For wealth certainly makes itself wings like an eagle that flies toward the heavens. Do not eat the bread of a selfish man, or desire his delicacies; for as he thinks within himself, so he is. He says to you, "Eat and drink!" But his heart is not with you. You will vomit up the morsel you have eaten, and waste your compliments.
Proverb 23:1-8

Consider the valuable lessons outlined within these words.

1. Do not allow man to be your source of aspiration.

How often do we do this? How often do we aspire to be similar to someone we deem important or famous? We become excited at the thought of dining with certain individuals because we think they are the greatest example of happiness we know. We used to refer to this as keeping up with the Joneses. In reality it is misplaced hunger and desire.

I could give you a list of men and women of God I admire, both from the Bible and from history. I could take a moment to talk about all of the great things they did to inspire many, including me. Many character studies and biographies have been written to do just that. There is only one Man, however, who is worthy of my worship and my aspiration to be like Him. That Man is Jesus Christ. I do not want to allow myself to be swayed by a desire to be like someone else, and miss the point of being like Christ. I fear this has infiltrated the Body of Christ far too much. We set up mental images, ideals of greatness, and have placed them as our benchmark for success. I will deal with this more in the chapter on Humanity, but the great men and women of God who are truly examples worthy of admiration are such because they chose to make Christ their source of aspiration.

My prayer for myself and for anyone reading these words is that we would be more enamored with and drawn to Jesus Christ than we are with any person or personality. Whether we sit at a table with any type of royalty or not, the best place to find ourselves is at the feet of the King! That is the hunger and desire that will lead to and produce eternal success.

2. Do not desire or set your appetite on material things.

It is one thing to have nice things. It is an entirely different story when those things have you. The danger is that falling prey to the latter is quite easy. Jesus warned about the rich man who felt compelled to build bigger barns to house all of his great possessions and wealth, only to have it all come to nothing. Jesus says *so is the man who stores up treasure for himself, and is not rich toward God.*[22]

I fully believe that God desires to bless His family. I also believe God has a hard time trusting some with His blessing. Often we live in pursuit of the blessings of God rather than pursuing the God of the blessings. The dangerous line then becomes using the Kingdom of God for our benefit and advantage rather than being effective for the King and the Kingdom.

Like anyone else I have wants and desires. There are things that I would love to buy or have. Many of those things I really do not need, but it does not stop me from wanting them. The balance is not making it my mission or pursuit to obtain those things at any cost. The balance is to not allow compromise to lead to justification in order to satisfy my own appetites or desires.

---

[22] Luke 12:21

3. *Do not weary yourself in pursuit of that which is temporary.*

I once heard Tommy Tenney refer to this as racing toward false finish lines. I cannot tell you how many times I have found myself exhausted from my pursuit of unimportant things. I have realized that when I put nonstop effort into earning a blessing that God wants to freely give me, I do nothing but sabotage His plan. The reality is that we all want to be ruler over much when God is simply looking for us to be faithful over whatever we already have from Him.

Paul told the Philippians that he could *do all things through Christ who strengthens him*[23], on the heels of his saying he had learned to be content with a lot or with a little. He trusted that God would care for and provide for his needs. How many people have labored and worked for things to the point of not even having the energy to enjoy them?

Again, please do not assume I adhere to some poverty mentality. I fully believe God wants to bless us, but I believe the design is that His blessing and favor overtake us as we are pursuing His presence.

4. *Do not partake in self-indulgence or be swayed by those who are selfish.*

Selfishness is destructive. I recently shared with our church that we need to see a movement from -ish to -less. Selfishness causes us to live in fear and greed. Selflessness allows us to live in faith and generosity. Our Proverb says that the heart of the selfish is not with you. In other words, the heart of the selfish is only with himself. There is no benefit in, for or from the person who only cares about themselves.

[23] Philippians 4:13

The entirety of the Kingdom of God is summed up in loving God and loving people.[24] A selfish individual will find it impossible to satisfy these mandates. When self gets in the way, it keeps that person and others from developing along the journey. May God always help us to direct our hunger toward Him, causing the selfish desires to melt away in the fire and heat of His presence.

Go For It

Those who hunger after Him *shall be filled*. When our hunger is directed in the right place it will be satisfied. When our hunger is directed in the wrong place it will leave us lacking. My son is five years old now. He no longer has long stretches of not eating. In fact, he seldom has a stretch of any length where he does not want a snack or something to eat. It is good to see, as it is proof of growth and progress. As an infant whether he wanted to eat or not it was on his mother and me to put food into his mouth. Nowadays, he knows his way around the refrigerator and pantry pretty well. He has learned the important lesson of feeding himself. Sustaining God's presence in our lives requires that we go and do likewise.

It is imperative that we learn the important lesson of spiritual self-feeding. Yes, we need to be taught by others, listening to the preaching and teaching of the Word. Yes, we need to interact with one another, hearing from the Word which builds our faith. Ultimately, however, we need to ensure that we know how to feed our own hunger. Just as each day involves food consumption of various amounts and styles, so too should each day involve spiritual food consumption. Let your hunger grow and be satisfied as you spend time in God's presence. Let your hunger grow and be satisfied as you spend time in God's

[24] See Mark 12:30-31

Word. Make your life about moments where you *taste and see that the Lord is good.*[25] The feast of the Lord's presence will always have a positive impact on your spirit, your heart, your life, and your family.

---

[25] Psalm 34:8

Chapter 4: Honor

We must never lose sight of the importance of honor. Jesus perfectly displayed honor from the beginning. As a young boy we find Jesus in the temple discussing the things of God with the religious leaders of His day. Although He was young, everyone was amazed by His wisdom and His understanding. When Joseph and Mary reunited with Him and shared their concern about His not being with them, He identified His calling and purpose. He explained that He must be about His Father's business. It would have been easy for Him, in that moment, to think more highly of Himself than he should, and to treat his earthly parents with contempt for their misunderstanding of His Heavenly purpose. Luke, however, records the reaction of Jesus as this: *He went down with them and came to Nazareth, and He continued in subjection to them.*[26]

A fitting summation of this is found in Global University's class on *Christ in the Synoptic Gospels.*[27]

No matter how much we know or think we know, no matter who we are, no matter how imperfect might be the knowledge or understanding of parents or other authority figures in our lives, it is still important that we have a respectful attitude toward those God has placed over us.

This statement should be applicable to any servant of the Lord today. The ability to give honor to whom honor is due should be found within our new nature. Therein lies the key –

---

[26] Luke 2:51

[27] *Christ in the Synoptic Gospels: Based on the Independent Study Textbook by Mike McClafin.*

within our new nature. Before we can truly give honor, we must first have a firm grasp and understanding of honoring God.

I find one of the biggest challenges in sustaining God's presence is not allowing myself to become familiar with God's presence and take Him for granted. That happens when we lose reverence for God's presence. In Exodus 19 we read of God coming down on Mount Sinai to speak with Moses. His warning was that nobody else was to break through to climb or even touch the mountain. Anyone who disobeyed this warning would die. He sternly warned that it was necessary for everyone to honor God's presence. In other words, God was establishing an eternal truth that each of us must be careful in how we approach His presence. Taking God lightly has never ended well.

Uzzah found this out the hard way. As David was attempting to move the Ark of the Covenant back to Jerusalem, those who were carrying the Ark encountered a bump in the road. Uzzah reached out his hand to steady the ark so that it would not fall from the cart. What he did seemed like the logical, sensible, and even right thing to do. He was not, however, honoring God's presence, but was choosing to approach Him in the wrong manner. Immediately God struck him dead.

*And the anger of the LORD burned against Uzzah, and God struck him down there for his **irreverence**; and he died there by the ark of God. 2 Samuel 6:7*

The judgment came quickly in response to the irreverent approach of Uzzah. Perhaps he acted in a manner God called irreverent because he took God's presence for granted. Uzzah was the son of Abinadab, at whose house the Ark was dwelling at the time David retrieved it. Uzzah likely lived in the house where the Ark was dwelling, but there was still an unfamiliarity or irreverence involving exactly what the Ark represented.

For someone to understand how to honor God, it is necessary for them to have experience in His presence. If that is false for them, it is necessary to be connected to someone who has experienced His presence who can instruct them in how to honor God. The next verse tells us that David was angry because of what happened. I believe his anger was more in response to his mistake than to God's apparent outbreak of anger against Uzzah.

David had spent years cultivating a life of worship and honoring God. He understood the value of God's presence. Those who were with him in moving the Ark should have been instructed by David about the seriousness of the task. There should have been parameters in place for properly handling the Ark of God's presence. David and those with him were celebrating the move of God without understanding the seriousness of or the guidelines that are expected to facilitate the move.

God is specific in how He desires to be honored. Following three months of the Ark being stationary at the home of Obed Edom, David decided to return and finish the move he had started. This time, however, he went about things in God's prescribed manner. We find that *when those who bore the ark of the Lord had gone six steps, he sacrificed an ox and a fattened animal.*[28] This was much different from before when the Ark was placed on a cart to be pulled by animals. Now the Ark was being borne by people.

It was never God's intent for the Ark of the Covenant to be transported in any other fashion. During their forty year journey in the wilderness, it was the responsibility of the Levitical priests to transport the Ark. When God brought the children of Israel to

[28] 2 Samuel 6:13 – English Standard Version

the Jordan in Joshua 3, it was the Levites who first stepped into the Jordan carrying the Ark, after which the rest of the Israelites crossed the Jordan River on dry ground. God's instruction demanded that the Ark of His presence be handled in the right manner. The only time we read of a different method of moving the Ark was when it had been captured by the Philistines and they sent the Ark back to Israel on a cart pulled by two cows.[29]

When David brought the Ark successfully to Jerusalem he did so in the prescribed manner, with it being transported on the shoulders of men. Along the way they offered sacrifices, offerings to the Lord, and they celebrated Him through worship. The first time around they acted with excitement and zeal; the second they operated in reverence and honor. As a result, God's presence was brought back to the His people and given a place of prominence in their lives.

He is Always Due

Render to all what is due them: tax to whom tax is due; custom to whom custom; fear to whom fear; honor to whom honor.
Romans 13:7

God is always worthy of honor. This word honor may be translated as *what has value in the eyes of the beholder.*[30] It involves recognizing the value of someone or something, and approaching and applying that value reverently. An ideal picture would be the woman pouring the ointment on the head and feet of Jesus. She determined that He was worthy of that level of honor and worship. Jesus Himself declared that what she had done would be remembered forever. He responds to and honors those who honor Him.

[29] 1 Samuel 6

[30] Interlinearbible.org

There are many individuals that I honor and appreciate, many that I respect and value, but Jesus is the only One I worship. I go beyond only respecting and honoring Him. He is always due and worthy, based on who He is at all times. I do not need a manifestation of His goodness to know that He is good and worthy of honor and worship.

Living and Leaving a Legacy of Honor

In February 2014 we laid to rest a personal hero – my mother. She lived a valiant and courageous life, raising eight children and helping to raise many grandchildren. Her life was built around investing in the lives of other people, and she did so with a desire to honor God through her efforts.

My mother had a plaque hanging on the kitchen wall with a message that is forever engrained in my mind. The plaque simply said, *"Only one life, 'twill soon be past. Only what's done for Christ will last."* That plaque epitomized the life and desire of mom. It is what drove her. It is what provided the wisdom in which she lived her life. That two line statement comes from this poem by C.T. Studd:

> *"Two little lines I heard one day,*
> *Traveling along life's busy way;*
> *Bringing conviction to my heart,*
> *And from my mind would not depart;*
> *Only one life, 'twill soon be past,*
> *Only what's done for Christ will last.*
>
> *Only one life, yes only one,*
> *Soon will its fleeting hours be done;*
> *Then, in 'that day' my Lord to meet,*
> *And stand before His Judgment seat;*
> *Only one life, 'twill soon be past,*
> *Only what's done for Christ will last.*

Only one life, the still small voice,
Gently pleads for a better choice
Bidding me selfish aims to leave,
And to God's holy will to cleave;
Only one life, 'twill soon be past,
Only what's done for Christ will last.

Only one life, a few brief years,
Each with its burdens, hopes, and fears;
Each with its clays I must fulfill,
living for self or in His will;
Only one life, 'twill soon be past,
Only what's done for Christ will last.

When this bright world would tempt me sore,
When Satan would a victory score;
When self would seek to have its way,
Then help me Lord with joy to say;
Only one life, 'twill soon be past,
Only what's done for Christ will last.

Give me Father, a purpose deep,
In joy or sorrow Thy word to keep;
Faithful and true what e'er the strife,
Pleasing Thee in my daily life;
Only one life, 'twill soon be past,
Only what's done for Christ will last.

Oh let my love with fervor burn,
And from the world now let me turn;
Living for Thee, and Thee alone,
Bringing Thee pleasure on Thy throne;
Only one life, "twill soon be past,
Only what's done for Christ will last.

Only one life, yes only one,
Now let me say, "Thy will be done";
And when at last I'll hear the call,
I know I'll say "twas worth it all";

Only one life, 'twill soon be past,
Only what's done for Christ will last. "

Only one life, 'twill soon be past,
Only what's done for Christ will last.
And when I am dying, how happy I'll be,
If the lamp of my life has been burned out for Thee."

This poem epitomizes the life of honor lived by my mother. My mom was a woman who in her unique way perfectly honored God. I owe much of who I am today to her life and legacy of honoring God. I used to become frustrated whenever mom would tell me or anyone else that when I grew up I was going to be a preacher. I promised her many times I would be anything but that. She would smile and tell me we would have to wait and see. I was confident that she was wrong and that I would have the last laugh on the subject. I am glad she was right; I am glad I was wrong.

My mother cared deeply for Christ. She sought diligently and daily to honor Him. She worked to invest that desire into anyone and everyone who would listen to her. As we were hosting mom's visitation service the day before her funeral, there were many who spoke to us about how mom had impacted their lives. There were many who shared with us about how mom had spoken to them about Jesus and their need for Him in their own lives. Her life was about honoring God. I am confident she heard Christ say, "Well done my good and faithful servant."

I honor my mother and the legacy she left behind; I live with the instilled value of honoring and worshiping Jesus Christ.

Practically Honoring God

How can I honor God? What does it look like? Jesus quoted the prophet Isaiah with these powerful words, *This people honors me with their lips, but their heart is far from me. But in vain do they worship Me, teaching as doctrines the precepts of men[31].* Jesus gives us some practical insight into truly honoring Him. We do not honor Him based solely upon what we do or by what we teach. Genuine honor is found in the heart, for it is out of the abundance of the heart that we speak and act.

Since 1997 I have personally been involved in some level of ministry. At various times along the journey I can recognize when the things I was doing for God were flowing from a heart that was in the right place. At other times I was trying to allow my actions to lead or establish my heart. My lips and my actions were honoring God, but my heart was in the wrong place. God wants us to honor Him by always keeping Him as the central focus. He is not enamored by what I do for Him. He is in love with me. I honor Him best as I love Him back, and as I allow the things I do to flow freely out of my relationship with Him.

I have found that in those times when I am serving or working out of a wrong motive, the ultimate source of my honor is self. I find that I am working hard to gratify or satisfy my own selfish needs and desires. A lot of energy can be expelled trying to quantify, clarify, or justify who they are in Christ rather than simply allowing their identity in Christ to serve as the example.

I continue to realize the best way to honor Christ is by being faithful. I can easily become so caught up in needing and trying to be successful that I forget to simply be faithful. He takes care of the details beyond my faithfulness. The greatest success I can realize is when I choose faithfulness and obedience over ambition.

---

[31] Matthew 15:8-9

Recently I sensed the Lord challenge me to consider the parable of the talents.[32] His question for me was, *How many talents have I given to you?* I argued that it was an unimportant matter. I sensed His challenge that it did matter in regards to my being faithful. I thought of a few ways in which I was currently serving Him. I also reminded Him I was waiting on His perfect timing to begin operating in a few other areas. His next statement stopped me in my tracks.

Show Me that in the story, is what I heard Him whisper to my heart.

I could not do so because it is not there. At no point did the master return to inform the talent recipients that it was the right time to begin putting those talents to work. He simply expected them to be faithful from the time He distributed the talents until He came back to call to account their faithfulness. I began to understand that the right time to be faithful to and honor God is always right now. Instead of spending my time waiting for the right moment, I would be better served to make the moment right now.

For years I felt God had called me to write books. For years I waited for the right time instead of simply being faithful to what God had called me to do. The understanding and freedom has come for me as I have found myself simply being faithful. I do not have to concern myself with success. I just need to be faithful. My objective is to honor Him and His presence. I would rather live in the sustained presence of God in response to my faithfulness in honoring Him than to find myself on bestseller lists or collecting life-changing royalty checks. In His presence He is able to bring to pass whatever He chooses, but none of those things will ever bring His presence. As the

[32] Matthew 25

Psalmist declares, *a day in Your courts is better than a thousand outside.*[33]

Where God is honored He abides. That is where I want to be. Grace is something that is given to us freely by God through Christ. His presence and favor come in response to our honoring Him. I am not dishonoring or devaluing His grace when I say I want His fullness. I want my life to be lived in such a way that He is honored, by life or by death.

---

[33] Psalm 84:10

Chapter 5: Humanity

Our humanity can quickly stand in the way of God's presence. Not necessarily in the manner in which we might automatically think, however. Yes our sinful nature will serve as a barrier to God's manifest presence, but we may just as easily block His presence when we try to separate ourselves from our humanity.

Regardless of how wonderful the presence of God becomes in our lives we cannot afford to forget that we are merely human. The presence of the Lord does not make us super-human, or suddenly transform us into a super-hero. To sustain God's presence, it is essential to maintain an understanding of who we are in Him.

Recognition vs. Submission

Jesus recognized His humanity, but He submitted to His divinity. He walked in the Spirit, He lived in the flesh, but He never succumbed to the desires of His flesh. The Garden of Gethsemane serves as a perfect example. Jesus defeated the cross during His prayer in the Garden, because He defeated His flesh and His soul in the Garden. He gained victory and peace in prayer, and was therefore prepared for the reality of what He was to face on the cross. He then taught the disciples the same principle to understand that their flesh was weak even though their spirit was willing.

He tells them to pray so that they do not enter into temptation. I do not see the reference to temptation as a reference to sinful temptation per se. I see it as a temptation to cease in the midst of the fulfillment of your journey or mission as given to you by God. The greatest temptation we often face is to save ourselves or to protect our humanity. The Garden of Gethsemane represents obedience, submission, and courage. Jesus displayed obedience to God's plan, submission to the will of the Spirit, and courage to overcome His flesh, mind, will and emotions.

Because of His understanding of humanity and divinity, Jesus both declared and demonstrated Kingdom authority. He knew Who He was and never pretended to be someone else. He never took the bait offered to His flesh or soul in order to boost His ego or self-righteousness. He simply walked and talked in Kingdom authority at all times. He proved that humanity does not have to be a distraction or a deterrent, but rather a perfect buffer when kept in proper perspective.

John's Understanding of Humanity

John the Baptist was birthed at a time in history that was ripe for something of supernatural significance: on the heels of what is known as the Intertestamental Period, where for approximately four hundred years God had been virtually silent. Suddenly, Heaven sent a man named John. He was born of pure priestly lineage. He was called of God from before he was conceived. He had a powerful mandate laid upon his life. He was filled with the Spirit of God while inside his mother's womb. He was the cousin of Jesus Christ. This man was highly favored by God. This man had a special place in history. And still he knew he was just a man.

As John was being faithful to his calling, many repented and were being baptized, but many others began to ask for his credentials. He began to be asked who he was and why he was doing the things he was doing. The barrage is best captured in John's Gospel.

This is the testimony of John, when the Jews sent to him priests and Levites from Jerusalem to ask him, "Who are you?" And he confessed and did not deny, but confessed, "I am not the Christ." They asked him, "What then? Are you Elijah?" And he said, "I am not." "Are you the Prophet?" And he answered, "No." Then they said to him, "Who are you, so that we may give an answer to those who sent us? What do you say about yourself?" John 1:19-22

John the Baptist was being questioned about who he was. The things he was doing were unconventional, and his natural position uncertain. Everyone was assuming John was someone or something special. Many even assumed he was divine. John understood who he was. His response clearly shows his understanding of his humanity.

He said, "I am a voice of one crying in the wilderness, 'make straight the way of the Lord,' as Isaiah the prophet has said." John 1:23

When we properly fulfill our role within the context of our humanity, others will be pointed to Jesus and be able to see Him. If not, they will only be able to see us. In our humanity He reveals His divinity. The rumblings among the priests and the public continued. They wanted to know why John was baptizing if he was not someone special. John maintained his position of being called in his humanity to prepare the way for the Divine One. Later, as the ministry of Christ was expanding, there were some who came to John to tell him that many were going to Jesus to be baptized by Him instead. The undertone was that John was being outdone by Jesus, as if ministry has ever been designed to be a competition. Rather than carry offense in response to Jesus being exalted, John again showed his understanding of his humanity and calling from God.

John answered and said, "A man can receive nothing unless it has been given him from heaven. You yourselves are my witnesses that I said, 'I am not the Christ,' but, 'I have been sent ahead of Him.' He who has the bride is the bridegroom; but the friend of the bridegroom, who stand and hears him, rejoices greatly because of the bridegroom's voice. So this joy of mine has been made full. He must increase, but I must decrease. John 3:27-30

I pray these words ring loudly in my own heart. I want to avoid the pitfalls of comparing myself with someone else, of trying to be who only Christ can be. I have been called to be *like* Christ. I do not have the responsibility to *become* Christ. The moment we forget that we are merely human before a holy God is the moment we begin to allow pride in our hearts. That pride can swell, build, and become the primary thing that separates us from God and His presence.

Spirit, Soul, or Flesh

The contrast between our spirit, our soul, and our flesh can be a huge barrier to allowing His divinity to shine through our humanity. How often do we hear the call to walk in the Spirit? Jesus did it and encouraged it. The first apostles did it and encouraged it. Paul did it, taught it, and encouraged it. Today we talk about it, but do we do it?

We have come to the place where we are convinced a person either walks in the Spirit or they walk in the flesh. That causes us to believe that as long as we are not pursuing and constantly gratifying our flesh then we must be walking in the Spirit. But is that true? How much of what we call walking in the Spirit is really walking in our souls? How much is driven by the soulish side of us – that which makes up our feelings, our will, and our emotions?

We may be free of providing for our flesh and the lusts thereof, but what about our selfish desires and our emotionally driven will? We can easily become tied to our soul nature, where every circumstance of life establishes our spiritual condition. Yet we call that walking in the Spirit. We tell ourselves to break through in prayer, but the feelings and drive of our soul may become strong enough that we superimpose our own will into our prayer and what we hear from God. We find ourselves basing God's leading on our own false pretense, and we allow our desire to become our word from God.

The answer to this challenge is found in God's Word. The writer of Hebrews says it this way:

For the Word that God speaks is alive and full of power (making it active, operative, energizing, and effective); it is sharper than any two-edged sword, penetrating to the dividing line of the breath of life (soul) and (the immortal) spirit, and of joints and marrow (of the deepest parts of our nature), exposing and sifting and analyzing and judging the very thoughts and purposes of the heart. Hebrews 4:12 (Amplified Bible)

The Word of God divides the soul and the spirit. It brings us to a place of reckoning. It causes us to have our minds renewed. It transforms our lives to a place that is beyond us and our natural ability. It brings us in line with God's will, as that is always found in His Word. God's Word possesses the power to move us away from our soulish, selfish desires and into alignment and agreement with His purpose for our lives. We often find ourselves operating in the soul nature of life because we have not learned to be content as the person Christ has made us to be. This comes from our striving to be something we assume we need to be. We must allow His light and divinity to shine through our humanity. As we talked about at the end of the chapter on Honor, God simply wants us to be faithful to Him, and to allow Him to work in and through our lives. He does so with our humanity as we submit it to Him, moving ourselves beyond the flesh and the soul.

How does a person know if he is walking according to the soul? Here are some common characteristics I have observed in those who are walking more according their soul than after the Spirit of God.

1. A person walking according to the soul will have a roller coaster life with high peaks and low valleys. The peaks and valleys will often happen rather closely together. This person will struggle with living on an even plane.

2. A person walking according to the soul will quickly neglect sound biblical truth that does not align with their will, desires or feelings.

3. A person walking according to the soul will pull away from or distance themselves from anyone who speaks truth that is opposed to their stance.

4. A person walking according to the soul will attract others by appearing strong, spiritual, and authoritative. In their opinion others need what they have.

5. A person walking according to the soul will assume their desires and wishes are the voice of God in their life as they have superimposed their will into their prayers.

6. A person walking according to the soul will navigate to and return to whatever gives them the highest peaks on their roller coaster ride of life. It is similar to a junkie looking for his next hit.

Again, the key is the Word of God, where we find the sword which divides the soul and spirit. We can choose to crucify or deny our flesh, but only God's Word can bring that separation from our soul. That is a huge step in recognizing, embracing, and effectively serving God in our humanity. I do not want to stop short in my soulish approach and miss what is available to me by walking in the Spirit. When I walk in the Spirit I realize and find greater freedom, for *where the Spirit of the Lord is there is freedom.*[34] It does not mean I become any less human, but I learn to focus my attention on God's power instead of my own.

It is Who You Are

This all boils down to where we started with John the Baptist. We must know who we are in Christ. It does me no good to try and be someone else. God has made me on purpose and with a purpose. Walking in the Spirit in my humanity is a recognition of and acceptance of that purpose. If I constantly live with questions and doubt about my role I will often find myself doing nothing at all. Paul gives clear insight to Timothy about his source of strength and his faithfulness.

You therefore, my son, be strong in the grace that is in Christ Jesus. The things which you have heard from me in the presence of many witnesses, entrust these to faithful men who will be able to teach others also. Suffer hardship with me, as a good soldier of Christ Jesus. No soldier in active service entangles himself in the affairs of everyday life, so that he may please the one who enlisted him as a soldier. Also if anyone competes as an athlete, he does not win the prize unless he competes according to the rules. The hard-working farmer ought to be the first to receive his share of the crops.

---

[34] 2 Corinthians 3:17

Consider what I say, for he Lord will give you understanding in everything. 2 Timothy 2:1-7

As long as we are trying to gather strength from our humanity, it will only be our humanity that we enjoy. If we surrender in our humanity, however, we will enjoy the fullness of Divinity as found in and through Christ. We must be strong in the grace that is in Christ Jesus. That does not mean to take the grace of God for granted or abuse it. It means we learn to allow the strength that only comes from God's grace to be the strength that provides and sustains our life. Through the strength of God's grace the rest of this discourse from Paul to Timothy becomes possible.

The way to most consistently *suffer hardship* is to have your strength come from a source that is bigger than self. If I am relying on my own humanity and my own strength, I will be quick to buckle and cower when difficulties arise. Proverbs declares that *if you are slack in the day of distress, your strength is limited.*[35] The only time our strength will be limited is when it comes from us, for the strength that comes from and through the grace of God is without limit. Followers of Christ are not promised an easy road, but we are promised to have Him with us, in and through all circumstances or challenges. The strength that comes to us by His grace enables us to suffer or endure any hardship. In our humanity, we recognize our need for Him. In His sermon on the mount, Jesus declared that the poor in spirit are blessed. The poor in spirit are those who recognize their own lack without the help of God in their heart and life.

We suffer hardship Paul says, as a good soldier. A soldier does not become entangled or involved in the affairs or cares of life, but stays focused on the assignment and task for which he

[35] Proverb 24:10

has been enlisted. His desire and focus is to please his commanding officer. A good soldier is able to face the hardship and circumstances that arise because he keeps himself in shape and training. He does not react to hardship or circumstances by putting his body through a crash course of training and preparation. He remains prepared so that when the moment of battle arises he is ready. In turn his commanding officer has confidence in him as a solider, because he recognizes the commitment level and trusts the soldier to be ready for any battle. It is never an accident when soldiers are chosen for the front lines of battle. The commanding officer is always attentive to his soldiers, watching the development and commitment of the soldiers under his command.

The entirety of this discourse is tied together when Paul says the winner competes according to the rules. God's outline is here before us in this passage, as well as consistently outlined throughout Scripture. As we follow the rules and design of God we will walk in victory. Too often we find ourselves in defeat or disappointment because of our choice to walk in our own strength and power. As we follow the plan of God, to find and to keep His grace as our source of strength, there will be no hardship or battle that is able to defeat us. A person who understands the war has already been won will not allow any battle to change the outcome.

One last thing I want to consider: Paul says that the hard working farmer should be first to receive of the crops. As a person works and faithfully does that for which he has been enlisted or prepared to do, there will be fruit and production as a result. Within God's design that person will be able to enjoy the fruit of his labor.

Having been a student of the Brownsville Revival School of Ministry I was always enamored by the magnitude of what God was doing in Pensacola during the days of the revival. I was feasting on the goodness of God in ways I cannot explain still to this day. One thing I realized shortly after leaving was that I could not reproduce the fruit that had been produced by the labor of other people. If I thought the seeds that had been deposited in me were going to naturally grow and produce I was sorely mistaken.

I learned that if I was not willing to do my part, find my strength in Him, stir up the gifts and seeds He had deposited in my life, I was going to be a crop-less farmer. Something even more revelatory and revolutionary happened, however. I discovered that when I did my part and began to see the crops produced from my own labor, it was the sweetest produce I had ever tasted. I am not implying that I have produced anything on the scale of the Brownsville Revival. I have discovered, however, that in my own humanity God has a plan and a purpose for me and that plan is to be productive. I truly believe that is what Paul was saying to Timothy. If Timothy or any one of us will stay committed to the cause, if we will find our strength in the grace of God through Christ, if we train and operate as a good soldier, we will be victorious and we will enjoy the greatest fruit, produced by our own labors.

In our humanity God is able to reveal His divinity. We do not have to cower or hide from our humanity. When we function within the context of who we have been designed to be, those around us will see Jesus Christ for Who He truly is. Just as John the Baptist, we can know and operate within the parameters of our role which God has given us. It is liberating to us and inviting to His presence. Who could ask for anything more?

Chapter 6: Humility

I take pride in my humility. Obviously I say that tongue in cheek, as that would be in opposition to the point of this key to sustaining God's presence. The reality, however, is that when displayed correctly humility is one of the most attractive characteristics to God and His presence. C.S. Lewis is quoted as saying, "True humility is not thinking less of yourself; it is thinking of yourself less." Paul said something similar to the Romans when he made this important statement:

For through the grace given to me I say to everyone among you not to think more highly of himself than he ought to think; but to think so as to have sound judgment, as God has allotted to each a measure of faith. Romans 12:3

To be humble means that we are conscious of our weaknesses and we are quick to give credit to God for what happens in and through our lives. Within the context of the above verse in Romans 12, the understanding is that we are ever being transformed by the renewing of our minds. In other words, we are becoming dependent upon God for who we are and what we are able to do. In that context, humility becomes the only real option of approach. The measure of faith that we each have been given is from God and available to all. It is our gift from our Father. It is not in our own strength or ability to apply or operate within that faith. Therefore, humility is a benchmark of those who are walking with Christ.

The natural tendency of flesh is toward pride and not humility. For a follower of Christ, the opposite is to be true. Humility is not a weak position to take in life. Far too often we convince ourselves that those who are humble are too weak to stand for anything. Would any of us consider Moses a weak man? Moses was said to be *very humble, more than any man who was on the face of the earth.*[36] This declaration was in response to Miriam and Aaron's speaking out against Moses. It was as if they were viewing things from the standpoint of a contest. Moses was not competing. Moses was being faithful, and he was doing so in humility. Listen to what the Lord Himself said about Moses:

Hear now My words: If there is a prophet among you, I, the Lord, shall make Myself known to him in a vision. I shall speak with him in a dream. Not so, with My servant Moses, He is faithful in all My household; with him I speak mouth to mouth, even openly, and not in dark sayings, and he beholds the form of the Lord."
Numbers 12:6-8

If this is the response of God toward those who walk in humble faithfulness before Him, why would we ever choose to do anything else? Moses is not our only example of this truth. Throughout Scripture we see that God lives with, walks with, and strengthens those who are humble. He *gives grace to the humble.*[37] Humility is attractive to God.

My wife and I are approaching fifteen years of marriage. Over that time I have found out things that do attract her to me. I have also discovered some things that she considers more repelling than attractive. As a man I would be foolish to continue in those actions which establish distance between her and me. I can recall some cologne that I have worn that has been effective and others that have been defective. There was one I had that was called Eau de Toilet. The name should have given it away. It

[36] Numbers 12:3

[37] James 4:6

was not an attractive scent to my wife. Quite the opposite is true when I wear any of her favorite cologne.

To go one step further with this illustration, let me say that I do not put on her favorite cologne in hopes of attracting someone else. She is my target. It is my wife's opinion and approval that matters to me. In the same vein if our acts of humility and faithfulness are in the hopes of attracting a favorable opinion from anyone other than God we begin to tread on dangerous ground.

Pride and the desire for recognition from man can quickly stop the flow of God's presence. Our acts of righteousness are to be done for God in humility. That is the type of person to whom God will respond. The Psalmist declared that the broken and contrite in heart shall not be despised or turned away by the Lord.[38]

God is Drawn to Humility

Humility grabs God's attention and moves His heart. I have found many times in my life that it is much easier and better to humble myself before God rather than to find myself being humbled by Him. Jesus illustrates it through the following parable:

And He also told this parable to some people who trusted in themselves that they were righteous, and viewed others with contempt: "Two men went up into the temple to pray, one a Pharisee and the other a tax collector. The Pharisee stood and was praying this to himself: 'God, I thank You that I am not like other people: swindlers, unjust, adulterers, or even like this tax collector. I fast twice a week; I pay tithes of all that I get.' But the tax

---

[38] Psalm 51:17

collector, standing some distance away, was even unwilling to lift up his eyes to heaven, but was beating his breast, saying, 'God, be merciful to me, the sinner!' I tell you, this man went to his house justified rather than the other; for everyone who exalts himself will be humbled, but he who humbles himself will be exalted."
Luke 18:9-14

What a pointed illustration by Jesus. We are not capable of justifying ourselves, but in our humility before God we are justified by Him. Humility attracts the presence of God. The Lord requires and desires that we walk humbly with Him.[39] Again, this does not mean thinking less of yourself, but rather thinking of yourself less. Often we spend far too much time focused on our strengths and abilities rather than being strong in that which God has given to us through Christ. In Chapter Four we discussed Honor. Often our desire is to be honored by both God and man. The recipe to prepare for that reality is that *before honor is humility.*[40] Those who humble themselves before God will be exalted and honored by Him. Those who choose to not humble themselves before God will often find themselves humbled by Him.

Others Deserve Our Humility

God should not be the only recipient of our humility. As followers of Christ we should walk in humility toward one another as well. Jesus told His disciples that if they wanted to be great they must be servant of all. He must have rattled their thinking when He told them that even He came not to be served but to serve.[41] How much of the difficulties or problems we face

[39] Micah 6:8

[40] Proverb 15:33

[41] Mark 10:45

in life are a direct result of our only looking out for ourselves and not considering others? Humility does not mean being a doormat or whipping post for others, but it does involve preferring one another. Humility means I choose to be a servant to others rather than demanding service be rendered to me.

The natural tendency is to feel as though we are entitled, and to live as though others owe us something. We find ourselves competing and struggling with others in hopes of getting ahead of them in a non-existent contest. We bite and devour until we find ourselves being devoured. How much does it honor God or His Kingdom for us to strive for victory in a battle that does not exist and therefore cannot be won? In the chapter on Humanity we considered John the Baptist and his response to this issue. His own disciples shared with him how Jesus was baptizing and gaining more followers. The undertone is that John should feel threatened by the success someone else was having in ministry. John, however, exemplified humanity and humility by understanding that as he decreased, Christ could increase.

If you and I are representing the same Jesus then we are on the same team trying to gain victory for the same Kingdom. From where I stand the competition that seems to permeate the church ranks is equivalent to what you see between fierce rivals in sports. Teammates may spur one another on and challenge one another to improve, but they will do so with the understanding that when their teammate improves the entire team improves. There is not a malicious approach that seeks to destroy one another for self-betterment and advancement. The encouragement from the writer of Hebrews is that we would *consider how to stimulate one another to love and good deeds.*[42] It

---

[42] Hebrews 10:24

should be our intention to draw the best out of one another for the sake of the Kingdom. If I follow Jesus, and you follow Jesus, we should be able to work in harmony. At times we may agree to disagree, but we should never arrive at the place of trying to one-up each other or to put another brother or sister down to improve our perceived status. These things should never be found within the body of Christ. This is clearly pride and not humility.

Humility Brings Grace

(God) gives grace to the humble. James 4:6

In our culture of grace abuse and misunderstanding we have this truth completely backwards. In our pride we say because of grace we may do whatever we want. Yet in God's Word He says His grace is given to the humble. The contrast is glaring. In the fourth verse of this chapter James declares that *friendship with the world is hostility toward God.* His grace is for His humble friends, not the hostile enemies who have befriended the world and the things of the world. It is through humility and submission to Him that He makes the full riches of His Kingdom available to you and me. James continues this incredible teaching with this discourse:

Submit therefore to God. Resist the devil and he will flee from you. Draw near to God and He will draw near to you. Cleanse your hands, you sinners; and purify your hearts, you double-minded. Be miserable and mourn and weep; let your laughter be turned into mourning and your joy to gloom. Humble yourselves in the presence of the Lord, and He will exalt you. James 4:7-10

It would greatly benefit us to apply these words to our hearts by living in humility and submission to God. God still calls us to live rightly before Him. Grace has not been given to us as a license to sin, but to give us strength to overcome and to be free from sin. We will discuss this further in the chapter on Holiness.

James calls us to humble ourselves *in the presence of the Lord*. Humility before Him does not stop when we find ourselves in His presence. We remain humble that we might maintain His presence. We do not move from humility to pride once we encounter or begin to enjoy the Lord's presence. It can even be understood within this passage of Scripture that to the humble God grants favor and the aid of His divine grace. Our humility is met by a greater manifestation of His presence and the power of His grace, exalting us to a new place in Him.

The lower and more humble a person is willing to become and make themselves, the higher God will exalt them and bestow upon them His grace. I call this the slingshot principle. Paul outlines this quite well in describing Jesus in Philippians 2:6-11. Jesus humbled Himself to the lowest point and has therefore been exalted to the highest point. The problem comes when we try to gain or earn the benefits of grace in our own merit or for our own benefit.

Rather than be proud and give God reason to resist you, is it not better to be humble and give Him reason to exalt you? Pride says I may be as God, do my own thing, and set my own rules. Pride declares that I may determine the best way to receive all that God has made available to me. Humility says thanks to God for His indescribable gift, for making me what I could never make of myself, and for helping me understand the value of His presence and favor. Humility means I want Him more than I want my own pleasures. God has made it clear the one to whom He will respond favorably.

Keep it Real

Before I close out this chapter let me simply say that false humility is poorly masked pride. A difficult lesson I have had to learn is how to take a compliment in ministry. The natural tendency is to say, "Oh, no, brother...It was all God." Friend, do not do that to someone giving you a compliment. You are doing absolutely nothing for them. They are taking the stance and approach that it is better to give than to receive. They are genuinely expressing appreciation for what God has done through you. We all know God gets the credit and without Him nothing of Kingdom value could be done by you or me. Nonetheless, the pat answer and stance of blowing off or refusing to receive the compliment is nothing more than false humility wrapped in religion.

My approach is simple. When someone tells me I did a nice job with something I have done for the Kingdom, I simply reply, "That is nice of you to say. Thank you." That prevents the possibility of placing condemnation on the person giving the compliment. It also keeps me from being openly or indirectly proud. Proverbs says that a man is *tested by the praise accorded him.*[43] If I allow the praise or compliments to go to my head God will reveal that to me. There is no need for me to take a false stance that does nothing to benefit anyone.

Plus humility that is fabricated is easy to see. I started this chapter with the tongue-in-cheek comment about taking pride in my humility. The reality, however, is that some appear to do that exact thing. I have come to the conclusion that open pride is better than false humility. At least with open pride the person is being true to who they are and that is a much easier personality with which to work.

[43] Proverb 27:21

I remember a horrible personal reality from my time at the Brownsville Revival School of Ministry. I had been approved to be a part of the Brownsville prayer team and, though I took that seriously, I allowed it to develop a level of pride in my spirit. I can remember having this air about me; a feeling that anyone I passed by should be able to feel my anointing. I talked humble talk, but pride was rising to my eyeballs. Thankfully God got my attention before I did something completely irrational or detrimental.

The world already sees way too much falseness coming from the Body of Christ. I have determined I do not have time to be anyone other than who God has made me to be. No, I do not have all the answers. In fact, I do not even know all the questions. I do know, however, that nothing matters more to me than experiencing and dwelling in the presence of God. I also know that if I am not careful my personal pride can be a block to His abiding presence. He responds to humility. He responds to the death of our flesh. He responds to our decrease by His own increase. Why then should I ever want to be anything but humble?

Chapter 7: Honesty

Recently I spent a Tuesday morning in absolute frustration and anger. I cannot point to a particular cause, I was just angry. My wife recognized it quickly and kept her distance. I was mad at myself. I was mad at the church. I was mad at the world. I was mad at God. I remember being in my office at the church and letting Him know just how mad I was at Him. I raised my voice. I slammed my hand down on my desk, breaking my watch in the process I might add. I let out all of the feelings and emotions I had been dealing with for days and weeks leading up to that tipping point.

I am not proud of the way I behaved that morning, but it did allow me to learn something valuable. I was being outwardly real in regard to what was going on internally. I was neither putting on a front nor playing a role, but I was dealing with the moment with honest humanity.

There was a day when I was afraid to be that real with God. I lived with this sense of fear that had me convinced I always had to be on my best behavior before God. Needless to say, that has all changed over time. I realized one day that the person with whom I have the closest relationship on this earth – my wife – has seen me at my absolute worst. The reason that is true is because I am that comfortable with her and that secure in our relationship. It dawned on me one day that if I was indeed in a close and personal relationship with God, things should be the same in that regard as well. I no longer try to hide the real me from God. When I am angry I tell Him. When I am sad He hears about it. When I feel disappointed or discouraged He is the first to know.

Do you want to know how He responds every time? He responds by coming near me with His love and His presence. Yes, at times He corrects me and redirects my emotions, but never in the condemning way my fear tried to convince He would act. At the end of my recent Tuesday morning tirade I humbly asked God to cut me some slack. I told Him I knew I had just acted childishly. I knew I had overreacted. I simply asked Him to not reprimand me in that moment. He honored my request, and I felt the genuine warmth of His presence come over me in my office that morning. I have come to appreciate how God responds to honesty. He responds with His presence.

I remember hearing a story one year while attending youth convention. The speaker shared how he had met with a mother who had recently lost her son in a terrible accident. As you may imagine the mother was angry over the entire situation. She had spent time in counseling, but nothing had been able to help her deal with her hurt and anger. The gentleman telling the story had spent some time as the youth pastor for this young man a few years prior to the accident.

The mother had reached out to him for help and he challenged her to do something. As the mother was sharing all of her raw emotions with this young minister, he simply asked her if she had told God any of these things. She was quick to point out that she could never talk to God this way. Much to her surprise, she was told that unless she was able to be honest with God and tell Him all of her feelings, she was likely never going to find the healing for which she was desperately seeking. Now she was mad at God and this young minister.

As he shared the story, however, he recounted receiving a lengthy email from the mother some time later. She recounted to him how after leaving the meeting and then repeatedly over the next week she had gone to her son's grave, told God everything she thought about Him, and told God how the accident had ruined her life. She shared how each day she felt a little better, but that everything changed on the last day she stood yelling at God.

The mother told this young minister that when she finished getting out her feelings she simply told God she had nothing else to say. At that moment she sensed and felt the warmth of God's presence for the first time in months. He wrapped her in His arms and simply whispered; "Now I can heal you." If there is one statement from this chapter I want you to remember it is this one:

God cannot work with what we do not give Him.

Honesty gets God's attention. Many times Jesus was moved with compassion toward the needs of people, and that was especially true when they were honest with Him. Many times He asked the person what they needed from Him. He obviously knew. He just wanted their honest request. If the blind man had requested help with a hangnail he would have been given a manicure from Heaven that he never would have seen. It is important to be honest with Christ. God has always and will always respond to a heart that is honest, broken, and contrite before Him. It is simply His nature.

Honesty in Calling

God knows what is inside of you and me. He is the One who put it there. Moses told God he was incapable of speaking well and was therefore not the right man for the job of leading the Israelites out of captivity. Nonetheless, he was the one God had chosen. The beauty is that when Moses shared these honest feelings God listened without judgment. All that is in us, those things we consider positives and those things we consider negatives, were placed in us by God Himself. God has never made a mistake; neither you nor I are His first.

Jeremiah wrestled with similar thoughts and feelings in response to God's call upon his life. Notice the honesty in Jeremiah's words as well as the sincerity in God's reply.

"Before I formed you in the womb I knew you, and before you were born I consecrated you; I have appointed you a prophet to the nations." Then I said, "Alas, Lord God! Behold, I do not know how to speak, because I am a youth." But the Lord said to me, "Do not say, 'I am a youth,' because everywhere I send you, you shall go, and all that I command you, you shall speak. Do not be afraid of them, for I am with you to deliver you," declares the Lord. Then the Lord stretched out His hand and touched my mouth, and the Lord said to me, "Behold, I have put My words in your mouth. See, I have appointed you this day over the nations and over the kingdoms, to pluck up and to break down, to destroy and to overthrow, to build and to plant." Jeremiah 1:5-10

God was not angry with Jeremiah. He loved his honesty. In response to his honesty, God defended his character against himself. *Do not say.* In other words, God told Jeremiah not to speak that way against His chosen vessel. Yes, God honors and responds to our honesty, but He will not allow us to denigrate His creation with our words. God also touched Jeremiah's mouth, the primary thing Jeremiah viewed as a weakness. If Jeremiah had chosen to hide his fear or insecurity how would God have been able to touch that area and alleviate the concern and doubt? We often live in hopes that God will automatically repair what is broken. Yet we often have not because we ask not. Do not hesitate to be honest with Him.

Be Honest with Yourself

It is also important to be honest with yourself. We all have things about us that we wish were false. That does not stop God from loving us. Neither does it stop Him from making use of us in spite of those things. The best way to live is honestly before God and with self. I have personally discovered much liberty in my life in those moments when I came face to face with my own reality.

I recall numerous times in my life where I viewed myself as capable of accomplishing things for which I had no skill or qualifications. I would work, force, and claw, getting absolutely nowhere fast, often even going backward. I would have to come to the point of doing what every man despises – ask for help or direction. Being honest with yourself is learning that you do not always have to hold it all together when on the inside you are falling apart.

God bless the men and women in Kentucky who were a part of my first assignment as lead pastor of a church. I made far too many mistakes and bad decisions to count. I did some things right, but the reality is that many of the things I did wrong happened because of my unwillingness to be honest with myself. The final example of that was in knowing when it was time to resign and move on from that church. I continually told myself I was not a quitter, and I could make it work. A precious man of God from the district office paid me a visit, and he helped me to see the honest reality. His words to me were simple. "Son, I cannot continue watching you die on the vine." I was desperately trying to hold things together externally; I was crumbling internally. Thank God for this man who saw that and spoke wisdom and life to me.

I vividly remember that conversation. I remember feeling relieved that I no longer had to pretend. As I began to cry it was obvious that he was right. In that moment I was forced to be honest with myself. I was no longer the right person for this position. God had tried to tell me. Yet, I was desperately trying to convince myself of a different reality, and I was unable to hear the truth. That moment in October 2010 changed the course of my life. By choosing to no longer live a lie, I allowed myself to embrace honesty and truth.

Recently I have undergone a lifestyle change in regard to eating, exercise and my overall health. That change has led to a complete overhaul of my clothing wardrobe. It has been a great experience for me personally to get into better shape, and has led to my feeling better physically and emotionally. One thing it has reminded me to do again, however, is to be honest with myself. This is who I am. I cannot change that. I may adapt and make physical changes to my body, but at my core I am still Rodney. I have started to learn to be more accepting of that all the time.

One thing I have forever removed from my closet was a pile of masks. We all have them. There are many sides to us that we want to portray, and we can easily find ourselves putting that mask on in certain company or certain situations. I am not speaking of anything psychological per se, but rather trying to be who we are not made to be. God has made me the way He wants. My job as a follower of Christ is to allow Him to make me the best version of Rodney I can be. He does not need to or desire to transform me into the best George I can be. He has another George for that. I can assure you that this realization is life changing. Do yourself a favor and be honest with yourself. Be who you are. Oscar Wilde once said it this way, "Be yourself; everyone else is already taken."

Be Honest with Others

Transparency is attractive to God and it is attractive to individuals who are seeking God. It is much easier to be honest with others when you are not looking to please them, but your desire is to please God and to advance His Kingdom. As servants of the King we should live our lives with nothing to hide. It brings great honor to Him and freedom to us. Paul declared in Acts that he did his *best to maintain always a blameless conscience both before God and before men.*[44] This happens as we are honest with God, with ourselves, and with other people.

A few years ago the Lord dealt with me about this issue. I had spent time cleaning out some closets and rooms at the church, and organizing all of the books into one location. As I was going through the books there were some I decided to discard. That evening as we were about to begin Bible study someone inquired about a book she saw in the wastebasket. My comment to her was that I was not sure how it ended up in the trash. That single statement of dishonesty haunted me until the next morning when I called this person to confess. She had a laugh about it and assured me it was not a big deal. For me, however, it was a huge deal. Integrity takes a lifetime to build and a moment to destroy. If I allow myself leverage on little white lies (which do not exist), I will soon grow into a full-blown liar.

Albert Einstein is quoted as saying, "Whoever is careless with the truth in small matters cannot be trusted with important matters." Little things count. Be honest in all things. Let truth be your compass.

---

[44] Acts 24:16

Honesty is the Best Policy

The real you and the real me will always manifest. When we are constantly changing our masks there will come a time when we put on the wrong mask at the wrong time. It would have been a bad decision for Superman to go to battle as Clark Kent. If he forgot to change his persona he would have been defeated. We fear that if we are honest it will reveal our weakness. For many reasons we have convinced ourselves that is a bad thing. Paul shared to the church in Corinth that Christ spoke to him that *(His) power is perfected in weakness.*[45]

When I work hard to cover up or hide something, I usually am only fooling myself. What good does it do to fool anyone anyway? We have been created by God for a purpose. The primary aspect of that purpose is to represent Him and His Kingdom to the world around us. When we are living a lie, we are not properly representing Him. That is why many times you hear the term hypocrite used in describing the Church. If I have to act differently on Sunday morning than I do the rest of the week then I do not have what I profess to have – a relationship with Jesus Christ. Out of that relationship will flow consistent honesty, representing Him well, and sustaining His presence in my life. If my life does not support what I say then I am better served to keep my mouth closed.

Declaring who I am does not transform me, but Jesus Christ is able to transform me into the person I declare myself to be. The more open and honest I am with Him, the more I allow Him to transform me. What I hide cannot be changed.

I was able to have my broken watch repaired. It cost me fifteen dollars and ninety-nine cents. It was not an expensive

---

[45] 2 Corinthians 12:9

lesson, but it was a valuable one. It will serve as a reminder to me that the best way to deal with my emotions is not through physical outbursts, but rather by being honest with God, with myself, and with others in my life. If not, a watch will not be the only thing that gets broken, and the repair costs will be much higher. My honesty will help prevent me from paying unnecessary costs.

Chapter 8: Holiness

Holiness is not legalism; legalism is not holiness. This chapter is not designed to delve into a tape-measure gospel that says you must do, dress, and fit within a certain idealized principle. This chapter is designed to delve into the much forgotten calling of God to *be holy as He is holy.*[46] God still calls us to live a life of obedience and holiness before Him. We do not have a right to use a black marker as we read God's Word. Regardless of what society or friends say about something, if Jesus declares it to be wrong it is wrong. If I cannot ask Jesus to join me and bless my activities then those are the activities I need to avoid.

This topic has virtually no popularity in our culture today. What is popular, however, is the idea that we may do anything we want, any time we want, in any way that we want, and it will all work itself out in the end. The anti-holiness, hyper-grace movement is akin to a wife publicly declaring, "Hey, does anyone want to sleep with me? My husband loves me and he will understand." We view that as ludicrous but view approaching God in that way as acceptable. The Apostle Paul gives an incredible analogy in his letter to the church in Ephesus. Listen to these words from him:

Wives, be subject to your own husbands, as to the Lord. For the husband is the head of the wife, as Christ also is the head of the church, He Himself being the Savior of the body. But as the church is subject to Christ, so also the wives ought to be to their husbands in everything. Husbands, love your wives, just as Christ also loved the church and gave Himself up for her, so that He might sanctify

---

[46] Leviticus 11:44 & 1 Peter 1:16

*her, having cleansed her by the washing of water with the word,
that He might present to Himself the church in all her glory,
having no spot or wrinkle or any such thing; but that she would be
holy and blameless. So husbands ought also to love their own
wives as their own bodies. He who loves his own wife loves himself;
for no one ever hated his own flesh, but nourishes and cherishes it,
just as Christ also does the church, because we are members of His
body. For this reason a man shall leave his father and mother and
shall be joined to his wife, and the two shall become one flesh. This
mystery is great; but I am speaking with reference to Christ and
the church. Ephesians 5:25-32*

The relationship model is crystal clear and beautiful. There is a mutual honoring and respect taking place, and that is the foundational design. In our culture today there seems to be little sense of this truth. This leads to the moral decline we see around us, which in turn leads to powerless Christianity among the people of God. Paul outlines some important factors surrounding our relationship with Christ.

1. *The first act in the relationship was that of love by the groom – Christ.*

There has never been and never will be an act of love greater than the one shown to us by Christ. He paid our debt to give us a life we do not deserve. That can never be understated. He laid down His life to give us life and a future. Sometimes, however, it seems we only view His sacrifice as an escape clause. He demonstrated this amazing love toward us with the intent of drawing us to Himself, to a place of intimate relationship with Him. When I in my imperfections show love to my wife it is not in hopes that she will make some other man happy. I show her love because her love for me matters to me. How much more true is that of Christ?

The reception of His love is not the end of the journey. The reciprocation of His love, however, is the point of the journey. Following His resurrection, Jesus challenged Peter to not simply receive His love and forgiveness, but to return his own love back to Christ by serving Him and serving other people. The famous *do you love Me* discourse is made more powerful by Jesus' calling Peter to do that which demonstrates his love for Christ.[47] As a point of clarification, Jesus did not demand Peter do anything to earn the love of Christ. He did, however, ask Peter to faithfully serve Him as an expression of his own love for the Lord.

2. *The purpose for His sacrificial love is to sanctify the church and make her beautiful.*

His sacrifice was that He might sanctify the church, having cleansed her through the word. His sacrifice was that He might present the church to Himself in all her glory, holy and blameless and without spot or wrinkle. This does not describe a decrepit, dilapidated, or defeated church. This describes a powerful, victorious, and strong church. This was, is, and always will be the picture Christ has in mind for His Body. The state of sin is ugly. The state of righteousness because of Christ is beautiful. Jesus died so that we may be a beautiful Church that no longer looks as she did before becoming His Bride.

Imagine a wealthy man finding a pauper woman for his bride. Imagine she owned but one outfit that was full of holes, rips, and was beyond repair. Imagine him taking her as his bride, giving her his name, bestowing upon her his riches, and giving her full rights to all that he owned. Imagine her going out into public every day with her new name, her new identity, and her new opportunities; wearing the same ripped outfit, going to

---

[47] See John 21:15-17

the same dirty places, finding her meals in the garbage, and giving her love and attention to anyone who might give her a moment of relief.

Jesus Christ has come to give us a new name, a new identity, and new opportunities with limitless options. Often, however, we continue to wear the same ripped outfit, carry the same old name, and indulge ourselves in the same dirty practices from which our Savior has delivered us. Paul says that those who are in Christ are a new creation, old things have passed away and all things have become new.[48] Jesus paid the ultimate price, not so that we could continue in our filth and defeat, but so that we could live victoriously as His Bride. The epitaph of Leonard Ravenhill sums it up well: "Are the things you are living for worth Jesus Christ dying for?"

3. *Jesus takes care of His body and desires it to be the best it can be.*

Paul says that no one hates his own flesh, but rather nourishes and cherishes it. We do our best to take care of our bodies. It is important for us to remember that the armor of God mentioned in chapter 6 of Ephesians does not come in all shapes and sizes. It is made in one size – the image of Christ. We are the ones who are re-shaped to fit God's standard. It does not work the other way. I fear we put ourselves into real trouble when we start trying to make God in our own image rather than realizing we are made in His. Sometimes, He has to adjust His image as reflected in us.

I mentioned in the chapter on Honesty about going through a time of being more disciplined in my health and exercise. It had become quite apparent to me that I was not

---

[48] 2 Corinthians 5:17

doing my best to take care of the body given to me by God, and was therefore not making myself fully available to Him because I was way out of shape. Between September 2013, and the time of this writing – June 2014 – I have lost over fifty pounds. Those pounds disappeared through work and discipline. It is taking work and discipline to keep them gone. There are foods I love to eat, but I have realized I do not need as much of those foods as I thought I did. Sitting on the couch is more comfortable than doing crunches or planking, but my soft backside had produced a soft mindset. My body is not going to naturally fall in line and do what is right. I have to take care of it and work to keep it in shape.

Jesus takes the same steps with us. We may resist those things He does to transform us into better shape, but we must understand the value and importance of the process. There are times when I read something in the Bible and think of all the individuals that should read and apply that particular verse or passage to their life. It is akin to me in my overweight condition watching multiple seasons of *The Biggest Loser* and being thankful that those contestants finally did something about their physical condition. In the same way holiness is something we can clearly see the need for in others, but overlook the need for in ourselves. As the writer of Hebrews declares:

You have forgotten the exhortation which is addressed to you as sons, "My son, do not regard lightly the discipline of the Lord, nor faint when you are reproved by Him; for those whom the Lord loves He disciplines, and He scourges every son whom He receives." It is for discipline that you endure; God deals with you as with sons; for what son is there whom his father does not discipline? But if you are without discipline, of which all have become partakers, then you are illegitimate children and not sons. Furthermore, we had earthly fathers to discipline us, and we respected them; shall we not much rather be subject to the Father of spirits, and live? For they disciplined us for a short time as seemed best to them, but He disciplines us for our good, so that we may share His holiness. Hebrews 12:5-10

These words are not popular. I remember a poster hanging in the youth room of a church that said, "What is right is not always popular, and what is popular is not always right." God loved us enough to send Jesus to die in our place, and He continues to love us enough to work in our lives to make us more like Him. My role is to allow Him to transform me.

My body is not perfect. I am not in world-class shape. Yet I do know that I am more confident in myself than I have ever been as a result of applying discipline and change to my body. I find myself treating my body differently now in response to the new confidence I have. I want that same thing with Christ. I want to allow Him to apply discipline and change to my life so that He can be confident in me as a part of His body. I want that confidence He has in me to be reflected by the sustaining of His presence and power in my life.

4. *We are one with Christ and the reflection should be mutual.*

In July 1999, my wife and I shared our vows of holy matrimony. I left my dad and mom to be united to this young lady with whom I had fallen madly in love. I took it upon myself to love her, care for her, honor her, and cherish her in every way possible. I put a ring on her finger and gave her my name, publicly declaring my exclusive oneness with her. From that day on I have done my best to fulfill those vows. I do not wander around looking for a replacement, and I can confidently say she does not either. It is doubtless that she loves me. I am beyond proud to call her my wife, and happy to know that she is representing me. I do not worry about her dishonoring me, harming my name, or harming my person. She has my best in mind.

The same is to be true in our relationship with Christ as our groom. It is difficult for a man to see himself as a bride. Nonetheless, we can understand the value of representing someone honorably. Our role as a follower of Christ is to represent Him as He truly is. There are many misconceptions about who He is, but the Word of God stands as our best picture of Christ. If we are representing anything other than Him we have missed the mark.

Holiness is Separation

The key to holiness, in representing the love relationship one has with Christ, is separation and exclusivity. Jesus deserves to be our greatest love and the recipient of our affection. I value my relationship with Jesus more than I value my relationship with my fleshly desires. I am not saying that there are not things I struggle with or that I never want to do anything wrong or sinful. I have determined, however, that honoring Him is more important than pleasing myself. In the chapter on Humility we considered James 4:6 where we are told that God resists the proud but gives grace to the humble. The height of pride in light of that is to say to God, "I know what you have done for me by sending Jesus to die for me. Nonetheless, I am going to do what I want to do instead of what You want me to do. I value me more than I value You." We take that stance and still expect or even demand His grace. Yet the consistent message of Scripture is this:

"Therefore, come out from their midst and be separate," says the Lord. "And do not touch what is unclean; and I will welcome you. And I will be a father to you, and you shall be sons and daughters to Me," says the Lord Almighty. 2 Corinthians 6:17-18

Our actions of separation from sin and unto God reflect our position as sons and daughters in Him. Our actions cannot establish or earn our position, but they do reflect our position. I cannot stress enough that the importance of holiness is not to earn what has been freely given to us in Christ, but rather serve as a reflection of and appreciation for what has been freely given to us in Christ. I choose to live right before Him because I love Him and want to represent Him in the best way I can with my life.

I am secure in Him and in my relationship with Him. I simply desire to separate myself from anything that might cause Him to separate from me. The sin of the world caused Jesus to feel abandoned by His Father on the cross. Is it not a dangerous place then to feel that our sin will never matter to God? If Jesus felt abandoned or forsaken, because in that moment the Father had actually abandoned Him because of the sin, how can we assume to be treated better than the Son?

The best definition of sin is anything that Jesus would never do. What would Jesus do? If we do not know, then perhaps we do not know Him. If sin is that which He would not do, it stands to reason that He would not be in the presence of sin either. If the goal or desire is to sustain His presence in my life, then it must include separating myself from sin and the behaviors from which Jesus would separate Himself.

An Unholy End

Paul emphatically warned Timothy, and all of us, of a last day's movement that would involve a moving away from biblical values in order to satisfy personal, selfish desires. The Amplified Bible makes it crystal clear.

But understand this, that in the last days will come (set in) perilous times of great stress and trouble (hard to deal with and hard to bear). For people will be lovers of self and (utterly) self-centered, lovers of money and aroused by an inordinate (greedy) desire for wealth, proud and arrogant and contemptuous boasters. They will be abusive (blasphemous, scoffing), disobedient to parents, ungrateful, unholy and profane. (They will be) without natural (human) affection (callous and inhuman), relentless (admitting of no truce or appeasement); (they will be) slanderers (false accusers, troublemakers), intemperate and loose in morals and conduct, uncontrolled and fierce, haters of good. (They will be) treacherous (betrayers), rash, (and) inflated with self-conceit. (They will be) lovers of sensual pleasures and vain amusements more than and rather than lovers of God. For (although) they hold a form of piety (true religion), they deny and reject and are strangers to the power of it (their conduct belies the genuineness of their profession). Avoid all such people (turn away from them).
2 Timothy 3:1-5 (Amplified Bible)

If we are not at this point now I shudder to consider things becoming worse. This is quite an alarming list. More alarming than the list, however, is how accurately it seems to describe the day in which we live. The last part is the most alarming: *Having a form of godliness but denying its power.* The purpose of the gospel is for there to be evidence of God having done something in our lives. The way I conduct myself will reflect what I believe. If I believe the God I serve is weak, passive, and powerless, then my life will reflect those characteristics. But if I believe the God I serve is strong, holy, and all-powerful, my life will reflect those characteristics.

It is not our image of holiness or biblical standards that are wrong. It is our image of God that is skewed.

When we see Him as the God of Heaven and the God of the Word, our lives will properly reflect Him as such. Until then we will reflect a shell of what we have been led to believe or what we have embraced as the image of God.

God's Holy Presence

The angels are constantly around the throne declaring that God is holy. They could be declaring any of His attributes, but holy is the one they cannot stop saying. As they are constantly in His presence the only thing they can declare is, *Holy, Holy, Holy is the Lord God Almighty.*[49] If His presence represents holiness then my best approach is to be holy as He is holy. I experience His attention and His presence because of His great love for me. I will sustain His presence by showing my love for Him, living holy and blameless before Him.

---

[49] Revelation 4:8

Chapter 9: Harmony

For years I have preached, taught, and stressed the need for unity. I still adhere to those convictions, but I have come to realize that we often have a misconstrued understanding of unity.

In many ways we wrongfully assume that in order for there to be unity among a group of people, it means they all must be doing the same thing. It feeds an idea that any level of disagreement to the established way is discord and division, and the person responsible must acquiesce or be shot. Well maybe not that extreme – but close.

How effective, however, is a unity that is forced? In what way does that genuinely benefit anyone? Unity from a standpoint of harmony has become my focus, drive, and desire. Let us define both words.

Unity is defined as "a condition of harmony." It may also be defined as "the quality or state of being made one," otherwise known as unification. [50]

Harmony in our context will be defined as a "pleasing or congruent arrangement of parts." [51]

What I believe is often called unity is actually a desire for unification. I agree that the whole is greater than the sum of the parts, but we must realize that without the parts there would be no whole. The whole is made better by the characteristics of the

---

[50] Merriam-Webster

[51] Merriam-Webster

parts. Therefore, genuine unity is a pleasing or congruent arrangement of parts.

In Acts 2 we are told that when the Day of Pentecost came the believers were *with one accord*. A look into the Greek of this word *accord* brings this important nugget to light.

A unique Greek word, used 10 of its 12 New Testament occurrences in the Book of Acts, helps us understand the uniqueness of the Christian community. Homothumadon is a compound of two words meaning to "rush along" and "in unison." The image is almost musical; a number of notes are sounded which, while different, harmonize in pitch and tone. As the instruments of a great concert under the direction of a concert master, so the Holy Spirit blends together the lives of members of Christ's church. [52]

This is harmony. This does not speak of unification or unity that is forced or fabricated. This is what we as the church are called to by God. The intent of unity is to meld together the various passions and gifts of each person into a common passion and goal. When genuine harmony is in place great things take place. Look at what the Psalmist says about harmony/unity in Psalm 133:

Behold, how good and how pleasant it is for brothers to dwell together in unity! It is like the precious oil upon the head, coming down upon the beard, even Aaron's beard, coming down upon the edge of his robes. It is like the dew of Hermon coming down upon the mountains of Zion; for there the Lord commanded the blessing – life forever.

First, let us consider that this Psalm is written in such a way so as the first and last statements of the Psalm establish the

---

[52] www.blueletterbible.org

theme or primary message of the Psalm. For this particular Psalm the theme is this:

Behold, how good and how pleasant it is for brothers to dwell together in unity! For there the Lord commanded the blessing – life forever.

What a powerful statement made then about unity. The Psalmist declares that the blessing of the Lord is commanded when brothers are in unity. He does not say that the blessing of the Lord becomes possible, or that the blessing of the Lord is occasional. The blessing is commanded. In other words, God is moved by unity or as we are looking at it, genuine harmony. There is something both naturally and supernaturally beautiful about true harmony.

Have you ever heard a skilled choir singing together in beautiful or perfect harmony? It is unbeatable. Now imagine for a moment, however, if each member of that choir chose to sing the same note rather than their part. Can you imagine a choir made up of only alto or soprano singers? That idea does not sound appealing to me in the least. Yet we often strive for, teach about, or promote that same ideal within the church. We want everyone doing the same thing, when that is neither God's plan nor God's ideal.

With the Purpose of Making Him King

The Psalms were written in relation to the life of the Psalmist, and this became intriguing to me as I was reading the Bible chronologically. Psalm 133 struck me the most. In the chronological Bible Psalm 133 is placed after 1 Chronicles 12. In that chapter something extremely significant took place. It is in 1 Chronicles 12 where David's supporters began to gather to him in Hebron in order to see that the kingdom was transferred from the family of Saul to David, as the Lord had said. We read that men from each tribe of Israel began to gather to David. David had served as king in Hebron, but he was about to become king over all Israel. The people of Israel were intent on seeing this happen. Listen to this:

All these, being men of war who could draw up in battle formation, came to Hebron with a perfect heart to make David king over all Israel; and all the rest also of Israel were of one mind to make David king. They were there with David three days, eating and drinking, for their kinsmen had prepared for them. Moreover those who were near to them, even as far as Issachar and Zebulun and Naphtali, brought food on donkeys, camels, mules and on oxen, great quantities of flour cakes, fig cakes and bunches of raisins, wine, oil, oxen and sheep. There was joy indeed in Israel.
1 Chronicles 12:38-40

What a powerful passage of Scripture. Those who were warriors *came to Hebron with a perfect heart to make David king over all Israel.* They took their place to stand with David based upon their gifts and abilities to fight. We do not see, however, that they made being a warrior a prerequisite for coming together to make David king. The next part of that same verse says that *all the rest also of Israel were of one mind to make David king.* All of the warriors and all of the non-warriors came together to do whatever was necessary to see that David was raised to the place of king. The Bible says as a result *there was joy indeed in Israel.*

The warriors were not asked to become peaceable. The peaceful were not asked to become warriors. They all came together as they were with the same heart and mind of making David the king. They came together in harmony. As a result,

David penned Psalm 133, declaring that the Lord commands the blessing when brothers are in unity.

In Matthew 1 we find the genealogy of Jesus Christ. The first part of that genealogy listed by Matthew is declaring Jesus as the *son of David.*[53] Beyond that we find fourteen other gospel references to Jesus being called or referred to as the *son of David.*[54] From that we see that our primary purpose of coming to a place of harmony is not to advance our own agenda or kingdom. The primary purpose of harmony is that through our unique gifts we can do our part with the intent of making Christ King, in the same manner as the Israelites did their part with the intent of making David king. Harmony is one of the greatest ways to see the kingdom transferred from the powers of darkness to the designated and true Davidic king – the person of Jesus Christ.

When we come together in genuine harmony as a "pleasing or congruent arrangement of parts," we will experience the sustained presence of the One we have sought to make King. That is the point. Far too often we end up with this ministry seeking to convince others they have the market cornered on the way things must be done. We are told that if we try to do something other than what they have proven to be effective then we are in the flesh, in disunity or sowing discord. That is simply a misunderstanding of the teaching of Scripture. God has distributed to each of us the gifts and abilities He wills us to have, so that through the expression of those gifts and abilities we can bring glory and honor to Him as King. As David penned, when there is unity the Lord's blessing is commanded.

---

[53] Matthew 1:1

[54] Matthew 9:27, 12:23, 15:22; 20:30-31; 21:9, 15; 22:42; Mark 10:47-48; 12:35; Luke 3:31; 18:38-39

The Beautiful Provision of Harmony

What then does this biblical harmony provide? We will stay in Psalm 133 for this answer. David gives a powerful illustration in this Psalm concerning the blessing of the Lord which results from unity. He compares unity to the oil that was poured upon Aaron to consecrate him as priest, and to the dew of Mount Hermon. The correlation is significant.

1. The Oil on Aaron

First, David says that unity is like the oil that ran down upon Aaron's beard and onto his garments. Aaron had been chosen by God to be the high priest, and to minister to the Lord on behalf of the people. With that calling, God had given specific guidelines for Aaron's preparation in becoming the high priest. The garments he was to wear had to be specifically crafted and worn, and the anointing oil that was prepared had to be poured over his head.[55] Until the anointing oil was poured upon Aaron he was unable to enter into his duties as high priest. The oil anointed or consecrated him for service, and to appear before the presence of the Lord. In Exodus 30 we find this description regarding the anointing oil.

Moreover, the LORD spoke to Moses, saying, "Take also for yourself the finest of spices: of flowing myrrh five hundred shekels, and of fragrant cinnamon half as much, two hundred and fifty, and of fragrant cane two hundred and fifty, and of cassia five hundred, according to the shekel of the sanctuary, and of olive oil a hin. You shall make of these a holy anointing oil, a perfume mixture, the work of a perfumer; it shall be a holy anointing oil. With it you shall anoint the tent of meeting and the ark of the testimony, and the table and all its utensils, and the lampstand and its utensils,

---

[55] Exodus 28-29

and the altar of incense, and the altar of burnt offering and all its utensils, and the laver and its stand. You shall also consecrate them, that they may be most holy; whatever touches them shall be holy. You shall anoint Aaron and his sons, and consecrate them, that they may minister as priests to Me. Exodus 30:22-30

This is obviously not simple oil. It is specifically crafted and designed by God to be used as that which prepared the high priest to fulfill his calling. Consider the ingredients used in the preparation of this anointing oil.

500 Shekels of Pure Myrrh

This is a free flowing liquid most commonly found in Arabia and East Africa. It is said that the best exudes spontaneously from the bark of a tree, but the inferior myrrh will split the bark of the tree. There is no question whether the anointing oil would have been made of the best or the inferior. To gather 500 shekels would be a challenge to say the least.

250 Shekels of Sweet Cinnamon

Sweet cinnamon comes from the dried inner rind of the tree. It is most commonly found in Ceylon and the islands of the Indian Ocean. Considering that 250 shekels is the equivalent of six and a quarter pounds, imagine the effort necessary to accumulate 250 shekels of this spice.

250 Shekels of Sweet Calamus

Sweet calamus is a fragrant cane whose root is the spice. This is most commonly found in Arabia and India. The strongest part of any plant is the root, and the root is the most difficult part of any plant to access. It would take great effort to secure sweet calamus as an ingredient in the anointing oil.

500 Shekels of Cassia

Cassia is the aromatic bark of a shrub found in various parts of the East. I do not envy the one that had to accumulate twelve and one-half pounds of shrub bark.

A Hin of Olive Oil

A hin is equal to about five liters and would be the easiest of the ingredients to gather for the anointing oil.

We find, therefore, that the oil was made of some fascinating ingredients. It may be said that any one of the ingredients used for this anointing oil was quite special and important on its own. Each carried a high value. Yet God commanded that these ingredients be used together to make the oil that would prepare a man to stand in His presence. To accomplish this would mean that the non-liquid components of the ingredients would need to be heated, broken, or crushed in order that they could become liquefied.

Note, however, that not a single one of the ingredients lost its unique value. The myrrh was not asked to become olive oil. The calamus continued to be calamus. They were simply asked to join together as they were in order to make something great. The whole was greater than the sum of the parts. In Exodus 30:33 God declared that if anyone tried to make any oil like the one He prescribed they were to be cut off from their people. Unity must be genuine. False unity is unacceptable. We must proceed with caution in our efforts to unite in order to avoid being cut off from among God's people. It is not about uniting on our terms, we must unite based upon God's standards.

2. The Dew of Hermon

The significance of this comparison need not be forgotten. Mount Hermon is 9,200 feet high and is said to be snowcapped throughout the year. As a result, Mount Hermon is constantly giving forth dew to the mountains of Zion and the region around and beneath. The dew from Mount Hermon is said to be plentiful even in dry weather. In the morning it would be wet as if it had rained. As a result, everything surrounding this mountain would remain fertile. Look at this vivid description[56]:

The mountain forms one of the greatest geographic resources of the area. Because of its height it captures a great deal of precipitation in a very dry area of the world. The Jurassic limestone is broken by faults and solution channels to form a karst topography. Mount Hermon has seasonal winter and spring snow falls which cover all three of its peaks for most of the year. Melt water from the snow-covered mountain's western and southern bases seeps into the rock channels and pores, feeding springs at the base of the mountain, which form streams and rivers. These merge to become the Jordan River. Additionally, the runoff facilitates fertile plant life below the snow line, where vineyards and pine, oak, and poplar trees are abundant.

The dew produced maintains fertility and fruitfulness. Along with the oil this is the other picture of biblical unity or harmony. It keeps things from becoming dry and barren. Biblical harmony will ensure that what God has planted will bloom and be nourished. Lack of harmony – division – will produce dryness, barrenness and problems within the body of Christ.

---

[56] Wikipedia

It Cannot be Forced

Forced unity is unbiblical. The only way is God's way and the reality is that He is not cookie cutter. He says this:

Now there are varieties of gifts, but the same Spirit. And there are varieties of ministries, and the same Lord. There are varieties of effects, but the same God who works all things in all persons. But to each one is given the manifestation of the Spirit for the common good. 1 Corinthians 12:4-7

It is for the *common good* that we have been given the manifestation of the Spirit. God's presence and blessing are found within the harmony of His body fulfilling their roles. They are not found within the context of demanding things be done my way. In some instances perhaps Sinatra's "My Way" should be the theme song for churches or ministries. The better plan is to do it God's Way as He has designed and instructed you.

Chapter 10: Hope

The writer of Proverbs gives insight to hope by declaring that *hope deferred makes the heart sick.*[57] A person can survive for a long time without certain things in their life, but hope is not one of those things. It leaves a person with a sense of emptiness and insecurity. In Chapter 1 we talked about the importance of having a Heart after God. Toward the end of that chapter we looked at how Jesus displayed compassion toward individuals first before meeting the needs in their lives. The widow of Nain was an example in which we find this to be true. This woman was dealing with a deep sense of hopelessness until Jesus restored it back to her. The second half of Proverb 13:12 says *but desire fulfilled is a tree of life.* The contrast is stark. To realize that for which we hope provides an ongoing source of life. To lose or feel delayed in our hope causes our hearts to feel sick and lifeless. Hope is a big deal.

I distinctly remember a morning when this became crystal clear for me personally. I awoke well before my alarm and felt a draw from the Lord to spend some time in prayer. I found myself in the church sanctuary on my face before His presence. The prompting had been strong and the reason quickly became apparent. I had been going through a time of frustration and strong emotional swings. In that moment I sensed the Lord challenging me to address the real issue. As we discussed in the chapter on Honesty, it is imperative that we are direct and clear with God in terms of what is going on in our lives or what we are requesting from Him.

---

[57] Proverb 13:12

I began to pour my heart out to Him, letting Him know that I was afraid. I was afraid that I was on the verge of either experiencing His presence in ways I had never before, or else I was on the verge of hitting a wall and regressing as I had experienced many times in my life. I shared with the Lord how much I could not handle to be disappointed again, and how hard it was to trust Him to take me to a place I had personally never gone. It boiled down to the reality that I was starting to see my hope deferred or possibly disappearing altogether. It was causing a great sense of anxiety in my heart. I began to see how I had begun to take control of my life, and how I was trying to make things happen in my own strength. I was slipping into self-preservation mode rather than self-denial or self-discipline.

I had been riding a spiritual high for quite some time and had become convinced that it was inevitable that God was going to do great things. Within that process I had found myself placing my hope and trust in the actions of God rather than the person of God. It happened subtly, and I had not even realized it. The truth is that Jesus Christ and His presence are our genuine and blessed hope. It is not about the things He does or does not do, it is about Who He is at all times. In Exodus 32, as Moses was on the mountain with God, the Israelites approached Aaron about making a god to lead them and to serve as a source of their worship. Their request to Aaron was, *Come, make us a god who will go before us; as for this Moses, the man who brought us up from the land of Egypt, we do not know what has become of him.*[58]

The Israelites were declaring that they were losing hope and trust because things were not happening as they expected. God and Moses seemed to be delayed in acting on their behalf; therefore, they deemed it necessary to do something in their

---

[58] Exodus 32:1

strength and on their terms. This problem is much more common than many of us care to admit. When it seems as though God is not operating as we determine He should operate, we begin to take it upon ourselves to fashion a god in our own image. Many times if we do not like or understand what God is doing or saying we take it upon ourselves to recreate Him into something we do like or understand. In our hopeless situation we begin to feel helpless, and our natural tendency is to make something happen. But what is the value?

The Psalmist gives great insight into the glaring difference between the Israelites and Moses. We understand why they each behaved in the manner they did by simply understanding this one verse.

He made known His ways to Moses, His acts to the sons of Israel.
Psalm 103:7

Over and again we find the children of Israel reacting negatively to situations, because they only knew God by what He did. When He appeared inactive they felt and acted hopelessly. It was common practice. They wanted to return to Egypt, they wanted to make their own god, and they wanted beneficial things to be happening for them at all times. Are we all that different? Do we only understand or approach God based on what He does or does not do? I declare often that I want to see revival, and that I want to see the gifts of the Spirit in operation. How often, however, do I allow those things to become the source of my hope?

That morning as I was praying I knew God was present, and I anticipated Him laying His hand upon me at any moment. I could feel all the anxiety and tension that I had built up begin to dissipate. Suddenly in that moment nothing seemed all that important. God was reminding me that the single most important thing is His presence and that any time I allow other things to take precedence over His presence I will walk in hopeless discouragement. In that moment I remember two Scriptures echoing in my spirit that must define my hope, my passion, my life. The first one was this:

But seek first His kingdom and His righteousness, and all these things will be added to you. Matthew 6:33

There is nothing else that matters besides Him and His Kingdom. When I seek other things, I may realize them at the expense of realizing His Kingdom. Yet when I seek His Kingdom first, I will realize that *and* the other things. The key is perspective.

Therefore if you have been raised up with Christ, keep seeking the things above, where Christ is, seated at the right hand of God. Set your mind on the things above, not on the things that are on earth. For you have died and your life is hidden with Christ in God. Colossians 3:1-3

God was showing me how I had allowed my affections to be placed on other things. Even though the things I was seeking were things of or from God, I was getting caught up in seeking those things more than seeking God Himself. I was setting my heart on the things of God rather than on the God of the things. The Bible tells us that where our treasure is our hearts will be also. My treasure was becoming the things I wanted God to do in and through my life. Just as we discussed in Chapter 1 on Heart, our real treasure is found in the person of Jesus Christ. When we need Him more than we need the things of Him *we get both*. That is how our hope sustains His presence. If we have nothing but Him we have everything.

Hope Produces Endurance

On multiple occasions in Scripture we find faith, hope, and love linked together. The most recognizable occurrence is in 1 Corinthians 13, when Paul declares these three remain and the greatest is love. That is not the only time it happens, however. These words are also grouped together in 1 Thessalonians where Paul declares,

We remember before our God and Father your work produced by faith, your labor prompted by love, and your endurance inspired by hope in our Lord Jesus Christ.
1 Thessalonians 1:3 (NIV)

We see here that faith produces work, love prompts labor, and hope inspires endurance. Faith, our conviction or belief in regards to our relationship with God, produces purpose. James tells us that faith without works is dead.[59] Sacrificial love and good will felt toward both God and man prompts us to toil and labor even to the point of fatigue. Love continues with the understanding that we will reap in due season if we do not faint.[60]

Hope in this context is that which links these attributes together. Without hope, faith will wane and love will grow cold. Hope is joyful. Hope is confident. Hope is the expectation of that which is good. Hope inspires endurance. Hope inspires a person to not swerve from their purpose even in the face of the greatest trials and sufferings. Hope is able to drive a person to great things when nothing else seems right. Hope sees what is possible when things seem impossible. Hope causes a person to keep going no matter what the situation may be.

---

[59] James 2:17

[60] Galatians 6:9

To Abraham God had given a promise of a son, and from a natural standpoint this appeared impossible. These words tell us why the promise became a reality.

In the presence of Him whom he believed, even God, who gives life to the dead and calls into being that which does not exist. In hope against hope he believed, so that he might become a father of many nations according to that which had been spoken, 'So shall your descendants be.' Without becoming weak in faith he contemplated his own body, now as good as dead since he was about a hundred years old, and the deadness of Sarah's womb; yet, with respect to the promise of God, he did not waver in unbelief but grew strong in faith, giving glory to God, and being fully assured that what God had promised, He was able also to perform.
Romans 4:17-21

Note these words, *in hope against hope he believed.* That stance led him to be *fully assured that what God had promised, He was able also to perform.* Even in the midst of a situation that appeared hopeless, Abraham stood on the hope he had in God. His perception was not going to establish his reality. He determined that facts were not going to interfere with the truth God had spoken. He embodied faith as the *substance of things hoped for.*[61] This same stance of faith is possible for you and me. We do not have to lose heart or lose hope in the midst of any challenge or circumstance. We can continue to believe God is able to deliver on His promise regardless of how things appear. We can walk by faith and not by sight.

Hope Overcomes Setbacks or Delays

In Mark 5 we find Jairus imploring Jesus to come and heal his daughter, who was at the point of death. How thrilled he

---

[61] Hebrews 11:1

must have been when Jesus began the journey with him back to his home. I am sure he was both hopeful and confident that his daughter's health and life were about to dramatically improve. His heart must have been filled with joy in knowing that Christ Himself was responding to his greatest need. Everything was about to change for the better. Those feelings, however, were challenged when the trek toward his home was interrupted by some lady touching Jesus. Why on this day at this moment did Jesus have to stop and address this simple, even pitiful woman? I can almost feel the anxiety growing in the heart of Jairus.

As the stalled moments began to mount Jairus caught sight of one of his servants approaching. His heart must have sunk as he noticed the look of sadness on the servant's face. He is told to bother Jesus no longer, for his daughter had died. All hope seemed completely lost. The excitement gave way to dejection. The anticipation was replaced by grief. If only Jesus would not have stopped. If only the trip had not been met with delay. If only . . .

Immediately, however, Jesus told Jairus to continue to believe. He was asking Jairus to have hope against hope. Jesus was stopped on His way to Jairus' house, but His journey to Jairus' house continued. Did Jairus wonder if Jesus had even heard what the servant had said about his daughter? The challenge before him was to continue to have faith. The challenge was to not quit believing even when the circumstances had changed. Could he do it? The answer was yes. And he was able to see the miracle happen right before his own eyes. Jairus was one of only six individuals in the room with his daughter when Jesus raised her to life. Everyone else was put out of the house because of their unbelief. I often wonder in my own life how many things I fail to see or realize because of my lack of trust, or allowing my trust in Him to be detoured. I pray that I learn to continue in hope, even against hope.

Hope Does Not Stop

Desire fulfilled is a tree of life.[62] This is the second half of the verse in Proverbs about deferred hope making the heart sick. This tells us that when that for which we hope is fulfilled it is for us as a tree of life. It is an ongoing source of life and sustenance. Let us go back to the story of Jairus' daughter. What is the first thing Jesus said after He raised her from the dead? He commanded that something be given the girl to eat. This is significant. It was not enough to receive her back to life. They had a responsibility to see that her life was sustained. How foolish it would have been to have the girl raised from the dead only to ignore her and not take care of her. That which is our desire fulfilled is not the end of the story. The ongoing life of the girl continuously provided the same level of life for Jairus and his family as when she was first raised. In other words, a tree of life does not just feed you one time.

We must live with ongoing hope. The same level of hope that we exercised to see our desire fulfilled is the same level of hope needed in order to see our desire sustained. In terms of the presence of God the same is true. If you desire and hope for the manifestation of God's presence in your life, you do not stop hoping for His presence once you find Him. Evangelist Steve Hill recently passed away and my wife and I watched his memorial service online. Pastor John Kilpatrick was sharing stories from the days of the Brownsville Revival, and one thing that struck me was his level of hunger. He shared that Steve Hill would often ask him if he were still hungry for God. John Kilpatrick said his hunger never waned, but instead he found his hunger for God's

[62] Proverb 13:12

presence ever increasing. On Father's Day 1995, as the Brownsville Revival was beginning, it was not the end or culmination of that hunger. It was desire or hope fulfilled, and it became an ongoing tree of life from which anyone who wished could continue to partake.

My prayer in my own life is that I never arrive at the place where I allow the trees of life provided by God to become dead, dry, rotten, or fruitless. Many times I heard my father-in-law speak of being satisfied with an unsatisfiable satisfaction. It always confused me until I grasped the concept. I want to always appreciate all that God has done in my life, but I never want to become too settled. I want to walk in hope and hunger for all that He has for me. I want to live with only one finish line in mind – Heaven itself. Until then I want to pursue all that God has with a hope that inspires endurance to see through to the desire being fulfilled.

As I shared in my former book *Just Keep Digging*, I want to be as Isaac and not give up either when it is tough or when it seems easy. I want to continue to press in and pursue until I reach my goal – His presence. Then I want to bask in His presence and partake of that tree of life each and every day. I hope to taste and see that He is good in ways I have never tasted or seen. When I do, I do not plan to push away from the table. I plan to feast long and to feast daily.

As I hope for His presence I will find Him. As I hope for His presence I will sustain His presence. When I find Him I will not let go of Him. He is my only hope. He is the One I love and for which my soul longs. Jesus, my hope is You.

Conclusion

When it is your greatest desire, you will go to great lengths to both experience and sustain His presence. At various times any one of these keys can become religious. That is not my goal. At various times any one of these keys can become a stumbling block. Neither is that my goal. My purpose in writing this book is to whet an appetite or fan a flame for God's presence. I do not have all the answers. I do not expect or demand you to be in agreement with everything in this book. If one statement from this book made an impact in your life then my work is done, and the time spent writing was worth it. If you disagree with me that is ok. The only book I adhere to and believe one-hundred percent is the Bible, so I do not expect this to be the second book about which you could make that claim.

Nonetheless you have seen a glimpse into my heart and passion. I love and enjoy the presence of the Lord, but I also take it seriously. I know all too well what it is to be void of His presence and it makes time in His presence that much sweeter. I have personally had the privilege of experiencing some great things in His presence: in private worship and in corporate worship. None of that compares to each new moment in His presence, however. I must not only experience Him, I must dwell with Him. If He is standing at the door and knocking I want to be the one to turn the knob and let Him in so that we may spend time together.

Is that your cry? Are you hungry for His presence? Do you have room or will you make room for Him? Is your hope found only in Him and the manifestation of Who He is? I personally cannot think of a better place to live or to be. With that said may we run with patience the race before us, with our eyes fixed upon Jesus, the author and finisher of our faith and all that we are or ever hope to be. His presence is available to you. Are you available for Him?

Rodney Burton is the Lead Pastor of Calvary Church in Carthage, Illinois. He is also available as a guest speaker for special services, conferences and events. If you wish to contact him regarding a ministry opportunity you may do so through any of the avenues listed below.

Contact Information for Rodney Burton

Website: www.rodneyburton.net

Email: rodneyburton77@gmail.com

Calvary Church
720 Miller Street
Carthage, IL 62321
217-357-2528
www.calvarychurchag.com

63045567R00065

Made in the USA
Charleston, SC
27 October 2016